THE EMPLOYMENT OF MACHINE GUNS

The Naval & Military Press Ltd

Published by the
The Naval & Military Press
in association with the Royal Armouries

Unit 10 Ridgewood Industrial Park,
Uckfield, East Sussex, TN22 5QE
Tel: +44 (0) 1825 749494
Fax: +44 (0) 1825 765701

MILITARY HISTORY AT YOUR FINGERTIPS
www.naval-military-press.com

ONLINE GENEALOGY RESEARCH
www.military-genealogy.com

ONLINE MILITARY CARTOGRAPHY
www.militarymaproom.com

ROYAL
ARMOURIES

The Library & Archives Department at the
Royal Armouries Museum, Leeds, specialises
in the history and development of armour
and weapons from earliest times to the
present day. Material relating to the
development of artillery and modern
fortifications is held at the Royal
Armouries Museum, Fort Nelson.

For further information contact:
Royal Armouries Museum, Library, Armouries Drive,
Leeds, West Yorkshire LS10 1LT
Royal Armouries, Library, Fort Nelson, Down End Road, Fareham PO17 6AN

Or visit the Museum's website at
www.armouries.org.uk

Printed and bound by CPI Antony Rowe, Eastbourne

S.S. 192.]
40/W.O./5715.

O.B./1432/A.

Not to be taken into Action or Front Line Trenches.

THE EMPLOYMENT OF MACHINE GUNS.

PART I.
TACTICAL.

(ISSUED BY THE GENERAL STAFF.)

This publication cancels the instructions relating to Machine Guns in :—

C.D.S. 36 (*June*, 1915).
S.S. 106 (*March*, 1916).
S.S. 122 (*September*, 1916).
40/W.O./4032. (*May*, 1917).

January, 1918.

PRINTED IN FRANCE BY ARMY PRINTING AND STATIONERY SERVICES.

S.S. 192.]

O.B. 1432/A.
40/W.O./5715.

THE EMPLOYMENT OF MACHINE GUNS.

PART I.
TACTICAL.

(ISSUED BY THE GENERAL STAFF.)

January, 1918.

PRESS A—1/18—4990S—18,500.

CONTENTS.

PART I.

CONTENTS—*continued.*

NOTE.—*This manual has been drawn up mainly for the use of the British Armies in France. It is intended to serve also as a guide for Expeditionary Forces in other theatres of war.*

INDEX.

PART I.

A.

B.

C.

D.

S.

T.

V.

W.

THE EMPLOYMENT OF MACHINE GUNS.

INTRODUCTION.

1. Recent experience has rendered necessary a revision of former instructions on the subject of the employment of Machine Guns.

2. Next to the Artillery, the Machine Gun is the most effective weapon employed in modern war, and against troops in the open at suitable ranges it is proportionately even more effective than Artillery, for the fire of one Machine Gun is more annihilating than that of one Gun or Howitzer.

It is therefore essential to success that the problems of Machine Gunnery should be appreciated and studied not only by Machine Gunners, but also by all those who have in their hands the organization and direction of Machine Gun work.

3. Unless the personnel of the Machine Gun Corps, both officers and men, understand thoroughly the branch of the Army which they will be called upon closely to support, co-operation becomes weak. Machine Gun officers, therefore, will receive instruction in Cavalry or Infantry tactics and organization at Army or Corps Schools, or by attachment to Regiments or Battalions.

The technical properties of Machine Guns with a steady firing platform enable use to be made of indirect fire, and accuracy to be maintained at long ranges. If full value is to be obtained from these powers, the personnel of the Machine Gun Corps must adapt the methods employed by the Field Artillery, in so far as they are suitable for Machine Guns, and reach a high standard of scientific knowledge. Every opportunity should therefore be taken of attaching Machine Gun officers to Field Artillery Batteries for periods of instruction.

4. The study of Machine Guns and their employment may be divided into three parts:—

(a) The technical properties of the Machine Gun, including its mechanism.

This part is covered by the " Handbook of the .303-in. Vickers Machine Gun."

(b) The tactical employment of Machine Guns.

This is dealt with in Part I. of the present publication. The matter contained in it is by its nature less specialized than that contained in (c): but it is impossible for the student to handle practically the problems of Machine Gun tactics, if he does not possess sufficient technical knowledge to appreciate the powers and limitations of the weapon, the basis on which the fire of one or more guns is directed, and the conditions under which in any particular situation the fullest fire effect will be obtained. Parts I. and II. must, therefore, be studied in conjunction.

(c) The organization and direction of Machine Gun fire, including the theoretical considerations affecting the fire power of the Machine Gun, a thorough understanding of maps and the instruments and appliances used in Machine Gunnery, and the practical application of Machine Gun fire to meet all tactical requirements.

This comprises Part II. of the present publication.

5. The distinguishing feature of modern Machine Gunnery is its offensive power. The offensive intention has always been present, but lack of training and technical equipment hindered its realization and led to the impression that the Machine Gun, whilst a powerful weapon in the defence of ground gained, could do little to assist the attacking troops in its capture.

Modern Machine Gunnery has reversed this passive tendency, and recent experience proves that the methods of offence now employed by Machine Gunners are viewed with confidence by the troops for whose support they have been designed. Therefore in future the Machine Gun must be regarded not merely as a defensive weapon, but as a weapon capable of supporting troops during an attack and protecting them against counter-attack during and after consolidation. In every operation Machine Guns must be organized, and their fire directed, with a view to developing to the full their offensive power; and in all training the offensive spirit in Machine Gunnery must be inculcated.

NOTE.—The terms " Machine Gun," " Barrage," and " Battery " are used throughout the present publication in the following senses :—

Machine Gun, to denote the 303 Vickers Machine Gun.

Barrage fire by Machine Guns is the fire of a large number of guns acting under a centralized control, directed on to definite lines or areas, in which the frontage engaged by a gun approximates 40 yards. (*See* Part II., Sec. 17, para. 1.)

Battery.—A battery of Machine Guns only exists as a tactical unit in the Motor Machine Gun Branch of the Machine Gun Corps. In the Cavalry and Infantry Branches the word is merely used as being the most convenient term for denoting a suitable number of Machine Guns placed under an officer as a fire unit for a particular purpose. (*See* Part I., Sec. 6.)

PART I.—TACTICAL EMPLOYMENT.

CHAPTER I.

1.—GENERAL CONSIDERATIONS.

1. The task which Machine Guns are called upon to perform may be divided, to speak generally, into two:—

(*a*) The direct support of Infantry Battalions by means of direct or indirect fire to enable them to advance in the attack or to assist them to maintain their position in the defence.

(*b*) The indirect support of Infantry Battalions by means of neutralizing or harassing fire, by which the fighting efficiency of the enemy is reduced.

2. The means adopted in fulfilment of this task may be summarised as follows:—

(*a*) In warfare of highly organized defences:—

Creeping or standing barrages, frontal or enfilade, in co-operation with the Artillery to cover the Infantry advance, and direct fire and defensive barrages to support the Infantry Battalions when they have gained their objectives.

Neutralizing fire, *i.e.*, intense searching fire on areas from which long-range Rifle and Machine Gun fire can be brought to bear against our troops.

Harassing fire.

Barrage fire to cover raids.

Direct fire and defensive barrages for the repulse of attacks initiated by the enemy.

(*b*) In warfare of improvised defences and in open fighting:—

Offensive and defensive tasks of the same nature, including tasks that have hitherto been allotted almost entirely to the Field Artillery, but for which there may not be sufficient Artillery available.

Against an enemy in shell-hole defences or in the open, searching fire will be effective at distant ranges (2,500—3,000 yards).

3. Accurate indirect fire is necessary in most of the above work, and, therefore, Machine Gun officers must be trained to organize Machine Guns for collective action in support of Infantry Battalions, both by indirect fire and by direct fire wherever this is possible.

4. When employed on the defensive the Machine Gun is a great economiser of men, for owing to its fire power it enables a defended line or area to be held by a minimum of rifles, thereby enabling the mass of the Infantry to be kept further back, ready for counter-attack or a subsequent offensive.

In particular, the fire power of the Machine Gun enables : —

(*a*) The ground gained in an offensive to be held by the minimum of men, thereby reducing the casualties from subsequent bombardment, though it must be borne in mind that if a Machine Gun be destroyed, a big gap may be created.

(*b*) A minimum of men, compatible with keeping the trench system in repair, to be kept in the line in ordinary trench warfare, thereby lessening the daily wastage from casualties and trench sickness, and the loss of efficiency through long periods of trench life.

(*c*) The enemy to be held on one portion of the battle front with the minimum of Infantry and Artillery, while the maximum of Infantry and Artillery are concentrated for offensive action on another portion of the front, where decisive action is intended.

CHAPTER II.

WARFARE OF HIGHLY ORGANIZED DEFENCES—
THE OFFENSIVE.

2.—PRINCIPLES OF THE ATTACK.

1. The Machine Guns available for any operation are most effectively employed when they are organized as a whole in accordance with a general plan, and allotted to formations in accordance with the tactical requirements of the situation. Machine Gun resources must be kept fluid, the work of every gun considered and a definite *rôle* allotted to it.

2. There must be co-ordination of the Machine Gun work throughout the whole force taking part in any operation. In a big operation the Machine Gun barrage work will form part of the Corps plan, and will be co-ordinated with that of the Corps on the flanks.

3. Direct fire over the sights at the target is the most effective form of Machine Gun fire. But although frequent opportunities should be forthcoming for employing with effect the direct fire of Machine Guns in open fighting in the attack as well as in the defence, the opportunities for using this form of fire to support Infantry in the attack of highly-organized defences are less numerous.

4. The offensive power of the Machine Gun has been increased by the progress made in the tactical employment of large numbers of Machine Guns for indirect fire. The experience of recent fighting proves that in attacks on organized and improvised defences alike, Machine Guns have rendered most assistance to the Infantry when they have been handled collectively and used in the main to give indirect fire, and that to resist counter-attacks the fullest value from Machine Guns is obtained by a combination of direct and indirect fire, part of the guns being retained in the rear to put down an overhead barrage on an S.O.S. line, and part being sent forward to support closely the attacking Infantry.

5. It must be remembered that while the Machine Guns always fight with Infantry Battalions, they do not necessarily fight from the same positions.

3.—CLASSES OF GUNS.

The Machine Guns available for an operation will be divided into two classes:—

(*a*) Forward Guns, that is, the guns allotted to Infantry Brigades to go forward in support of the attacking Battalions, and carry out consolidation in depth of the ground won. These guns are definitely under the control of the Brigade Commander.

(*b*) Rear Guns, that is, the guns which supply barrage and other forms of covering fire from positions in rear.

In addition, the question of holding some guns in reserve should always be considered, both by Divisional and by Brigade Commanders.

4.—ROLE OF FORWARD GUNS.

1. The *rôle* of every gun will be laid down in orders, namely, the location at zero, the route of advance, the final locality from which it is to be employed, the nature of that employment, and the Report Centres through which orders will reach the commanders of Forward Guns.

The use of aeroplane photographs, both vertical and oblique, are of great assistance in selecting routes, forward dumps, etc.

2. Apart from exceptional circumstances, such as when they form part of a detached force, these guns should not be definitely attached to Infantry Battalions.

The Machine Gun is not a suitable weapon to send forward tied to an Infantry Battalion, for the following reasons:—

(*a*) Its weight, which makes it practically impossible for the Machine Gunner to keep up with the Battalion. Even if he succeeds in doing so, he becomes too exhausted to be useful until some time has elapsed.

(*b*) Its visibility, as compared with the Lewis Gun, which makes it difficult at short notice to find a concealed fire position.

(*c*) Now that the Infantry Battalion has a large number of Lewis Guns, the necessity for attaching Machine Guns to it has ceased to exist. The Lewis Gun and other Battalion weapons are usually sufficient for repelling early local counter-attacks. Machine Guns should aim at getting into their defence positions in time for the " setpiece " counter-attacks which come later.

11

3. Too many Machine Guns should not be pushed forward into the advanced portions of the captured position for early organization for defence, as this only results in useless loss of personnel and material, and in reducing the number of guns available for the S.O.S. barrage by which the Infantry are protected during organization.

4. The guns will usually work in sub-sections of two guns, each sub-section being under an officer.

5. The location of the guns at Zero will be chosen with regard to the line on which the hostile barrage will most probably first descend. They should as a rule do no firing before their advance. Thus they will be packed up and their personnel fresh when the time to move forward arrives. An exception to this would be guns taking part in a barrage during the earlier phases of an attack and being picked up by troops passing through to take part in a later phase of the operations.

6. In order that they may not become mixed in the *melée*, they will not follow the attacking waves too closely. The advance will be by "bounds" along previously selected routes. The halting place at the end of each "bound" will be given in advance, and should not be in proximity to any prominent landmark.

7. The localities from which the guns are to be employed finally will be laid down in orders, and representatives of the Forward Guns, preceded by their Scouts, will reconnoitre these localities and choose the actual position of each gun.

8. There are two ways of conducting this reconnaissance, by:—

(a) Each "bound" being reconnoitred separately.

(b) Representatives going forward with the Infantry to the final localities, and sending back for the guns when they are required.

9. It is usually best to cross No Man's Land early, so as to avoid the enemy barrage, and to make the enemy front or support lines the first halt. The guns will not leave the last halt to move forward to their final localities until the final position for each gun has been selected. They will then be guided direct to the positions from which they will come into action.

10. Open emplacements should, when possible, be prepared for them, before they are brought up.

11. The guns, both in their intermediate and final locations, will be distributed in depth.

12. Each sub-section of Forward Guns will be allotted a Report Centre, which normally will be the Headquarters of the Battalion in whose area they are operating. The commander of the sub-section will have runners at his Report Centre, so that messages can reach him, if he is not there himself at the time. The sub-section commander will report to the Battalion Commander in whose area he is operating, when his guns have taken up their allotted positions.

13. The Forward Machine Guns allotted to the consolidation will devote all their energy to the organization of their defensive positions, and in principle will not engage unimportant scattered parties of the enemy, or fire on hostile aircraft.

14. When the ground is favourable, *" Batteries of opportunity,"* consisting of not more than four Machine Guns* under the command of an officer, will move forward so as to reach points from which good forward observation is obtainable, early after the capture of the final objective.

15. The object of these Batteries is to seize every opportunity of inflicting loss on the enemy. They will:—

(a) Give close support by direct fire to the infantry during counter-attacks.

(b) Supplement and stiffen the system of defence of the area newly captured.

(c) Engage hostile artillery or bodies of troops within range.

(d) Engage hostile planes flying low.

16. The Batteries of opportunity must be handled with great boldness, and the largest initiative must be left to the Commanders regarding the selection of their position and the method of carrying out their task.

17. More than two Batteries of opportunity for a Division will seldom be required; the sector of activity of each Battery so employed will be allotted by the Division, and when more than a Division is engaged the employment of these Batteries will be co-ordinated by the Corps.

18. The Batteries of opportunity will inform the nearest Infantry Commander of their whereabouts, and will, when possible, work in co-operation with the nearest Artillery O.P.

* Experiments have proved that the fire of single Machine Guns at medium or long range is too scattered to be effective, and that the fire unit for long and medium range must consist of four Machine Guns.

5.—ROLE OF REAR GUNS.

1. The object of barrage fire by Machine Guns is two-fold: to assist the Infantry during an advance and to protect them during the organization of the captured position.

During an advance Machine Gun fire should be applied continuously either along the whole front under attack or on areas selected in advance by the General Staff. In the storm of a battle it is impossible to engage in detail the enemy targets ahead of the advancing line, and therefore it is necessary to sweep systematically all ground which may contain these targets. Similarly, after a successful advance, when the assaulting troops are in unfamiliar surroundings, ignorant of the exact disposition of their resources, and exhausted by the physical and nervous strain of their recent effort, and when organization of the captured position is not sufficiently advanced to be of great value in repelling a counter-attack, the Infantry's power of resistance must be strengthened by fire from the rear, which is applied the moment it is called for and on as wide a front as the counter-attack demands.

2. The Infantry advance will be covered by:—

(*a*) Standing barrages, placed on or beyond the various objectives to be attacked, and remaining there until such time as the Infantry advance renders it necessary for them to be placed further forward; or

(*b*) Creeping barrages, moving in front of the 18-pdr. creeping barrage and intensifying its effect; the Machine Gun lifts being not less than 100 yards. This is the more thorough method and, when time and resources permit, the more effective.

The covering barrages will, where necessary, be supplemented by, or may, on occasions (the controlling factor being the density of the artillery barrage), take the form of:—

(*a*) Standing barrages, placed on enemy lines of communication, likely approaches for enemy counter-attacks, and open ground over which the enemy must retire or be reinforced.

(*b*) Neutralizing fire, placed on commanding ground, or other areas from which observation can be obtained and fire directed by the enemy on our Infantry.

(*c*) Neutralizing fire, placed on positions which, though not being directly attacked at the time, are being enveloped or are holding up an attack already in progress.

3. During organization for defence the troops will be protected by S.O.S. barrages, arranged to go down as close in front of the line which is being organized as is consistent with the safety of the troops occupying it.

4. The direction from which barrage fire can be applied is either frontal, flanking or enfilade, but as enfilade fire is a form of flanking fire, it is only necessary to compare frontal with flanking barrages.

FRONTAL BARRAGE :—

Advantages :—It is usually the only one possible to employ on a general scale for covering the attacking troops in a big operation; it gives a greater depth of beaten zone; that is to say, the attacker walks up the cone instead of across it; it is simple to arrange and carry out.

Disadvantages :—It requires more guns to cover a given front; it cannot be placed so close to the attacking troops.

FLANKING BARRAGE:—

Advantages :—It can be placed rather closer to the Infantry; it requires fewer guns to cover a given front; it is more effective against trenches and streets which run at right angles to the general line of advance; it is especially suitable for the protection of an exposed flank.

Disadvantages :—It is seldom possible, except in small operations, or in operations where one portion of the line is in advance of that from which the attack is being made; it gives a narrower beaten zone, and is therefore more quickly traversed by the attacker; it is more difficult to arrange and carry out.

It can therefore be concluded that the frontal barrage will be the normal type of barrage for covering the advance of the Infantry and forming the S.O.S. barrage line; but that, when sufficient guns are available and the conformation of the line permits, a combination of frontal and flanking barrages will be the surest means of obtaining the fullest effect from the fire of Machine Guns.

5. When the ground is exceptionally favourable or has buildings on it, it is sometimes possible to use direct fire for covering the advance of troops. As a rule, however, if much Artillery is being employed, the dust renders observation impossible. Attacks frequently take place in the half-light of

early dawn, namely, at an hour when, owing to darkness or morning mist, it is not possible to see over the sights, and the control of a large number of guns by any means except that of the time-table is out of the question.

6. The Rear Guns, especially those forming the S.O.S. barrage line, form a strong rear line of defence in the event of the enemy breaking through, and at the same time a protection to our own Artillery and a reserve of power available to meet any new situation that may arise.

6.—ORGANIZATION OF REAR GUNS.

1. In a big operation the general plan will be drawn up by the Corps, in order that all the available Machine Guns may be used in the most effective manner and that the necessary co-operation with neighbouring Divisions and Corps may be assured. The same care must be taken to co-ordinate the Machine Gun barrages on neighbouring fronts as is taken with the Artillery barrages. The creeping barrage of the Machine Guns should be simple, and complicated lifts and changes of direction avoided.

2. The general plan having been drawn up and the Divisional Machine Gun Commanders conferred with, they in their turn will organize the guns at their disposal in accordance with that plan.

3. At the Divisional Conference the Divisional Commander, in consultation with the Brigade Commanders and the Divisional Machine Gun Commander, will have decided on the number of guns to be allotted to each category, and on the proportion of guns and personnel to be kept in reserve to replace casualties and to carry out reliefs.

4. The Rear Guns will be divided into Groups, usually one Group to each Brigade front. This will facilitate communication and ensure the Commander of a Group being in close touch with the Commander of the Brigade which he is supporting. Each Group will be sub-divided into "Batteries."* If the number of Batteries in any one Group exceeds four, it may be convenient for the sake of control to form sub-groups. The normal number of guns in a Battery is eight; it may be less, *i.e.*, four or six, but owing to difficulties of control should not be more.

---

* *See* note at end of Introduction.

16

5. Each Group will be under the command of an officer appointed as " Group Commander." It is essential that he should have his Headquarters at the Headquarters of the Brigade whose area his Group is covering.

He will be in telephonic communication with his Batteries, and will arrange for this communication to be duplicated by visual signalling whenever possible.

6. Each Battery will be under the command of an officer appointed as " Battery Commander."

7. In each Battery there should be at least one officer to four guns, and one N.C.O. not below the rank of Corporal to two guns. The Battery Commander is responsible that proper control is exercised throughout his Battery.

8. The Divisional Machine Gun Commander will be in close touch with Divisional Headquarters. He will be in communication with his Group Commanders, and also with the officer on the Corps Staff who is co-ordinating the operations of the Machine Guns.

7.—ORGANIZATION OF FORWARD AND REAR GUNS IN A DIVISION.

1. The tasks of the Forward Guns will be allotted by the Brigade Commander according to the tactical requirements.

2. If it is desired to increase the number of Rear Guns, it is sometimes possible to arrange that the formations which go through to the further objectives shall lend guns for barrage work during the earlier phases of the operation, and pick them up as they pass through, provided always that the combination of tasks does not render the personnel unfit for energetic action in their final forward position.

3. As a general rule, each Rear. Gun will be allotted a frontage of 40 yards per gun with a closer concentration on points which require special attention.

8.—HARASSING FIRE.

1. The object of harassing fire is to prevent overland movement by the enemy and to dislocate the supply and maintenance of his front system. The fire will usually be at night. An organized scheme for carrying it out will be put in operation a certain number of days before an attack, and maintained in intensity until Zero day.

2. The original plan and the daily programme will be submitted to the Divisional Commander by the Divisional Machine Gun Commander, in co-operation with the Divisional Artillery Staff, and will be co-ordinated by the Corps. In order to secure a proper division of work, the Machine Gun plan of harassing fire should be part of a general scheme embracing the operations of Artillery, Machine Guns and Trench Mortars. Co-operation with the Intelligence (G.S.O.3) will ensure that the harassing scheme is kept up to date as regards " nerve centres " in the enemy's lines.

3. Key maps should be issued to Machine Gun Officers in charge of guns engaged in harassing fire. This reduces greatly the delay in getting out the daily fire programme.

4. For details of target and types of fire *see* Part II.

9.—SITING OF REAR GUNS.

1. Guns must be carefully sited in inconspicuous places. When the positions are in view of the enemy, the emplacements must be dug by night and kept camouflaged during the day. If the terrain is very exposed it may be inadvisable to dig any emplacements before Zero night, the ground being merely pegged out in advance. For specimens of emplacements used in recent offensive operations *see* Appendix II.

2. Care must be taken to avoid movement near the Battery positions by day, and the making of beaten tracks leading up to them, tracks being very visible on aeroplane photographs.

3. Once the battle has begun, it is often no longer possible, except in very favourable conditions, to conceal the Battery positions, and the success of the battle must be relied on to prevent the enemy being able to divert sufficient Artillery from his original programme to deal effectively with the Rear Guns.

4. Precautions should be taken against low flying aeroplanes. Machine Gun detachments are responsible for their own protection, but Lewis Guns, posted away from the Battery positions but within range of such aircraft, would prove valuable for protecting Rear Guns during the battle, if available.

10.—FORWARD MOVEMENT OF BATTERIES.

1. The arrangements for the forward movement of a large number of Batteries, with the necessary ammunition, spare parts, water, oil, etc., are complicated; and Divisional Machine

Gun Commanders are responsible for preparing the detailed instructions for the forward moves of the Batteries forming the Groups under their command.

2. Time of starting, route, halting places, final location, will be given to each Battery, and maps prepared showing all details.

In addition, the calculations necessary to enable the Batteries to open fire from their new positions in the shortest possible time will be worked out beforehand, and the necessary fire órders and fire organization tables issued. Oblique aeroplane photographs should be supplied to all Batteries moving forward.

3. Wherever possible pack animals should be used to assist the Batteries in their forward move. It may sometimes be advisable to place the pack animals, while they are waiting for the time to advance, in pits which have been dug in rear of the Battery, but not so close as to disclose its position.

4. Whether pack animals are used or not, Batteries require assistance from the Infantry on the scale of two extra carriers per gun. These must be picked men, selected for their physical strength and staying power, and they should be attached to the Machine Gun Companies for some time beforehand in order that they may be trained in their duties.

5. All forward moves should be rehearsed beforehand over ground which resembles as nearly as possible that actually to be crossed.

During these practices and at other times the personnel will be trained in the carrying of their loads for long distances, and everything possible will be done to increase their fitness for the task that they will have to perform.

11.—FINAL S.O.S. BARRAGE.

1. This should be arranged so as to provide a complete belt of fire along the whole front of the operation.

If the operation is one in which the length of the advance makes it necessary for the Artillery, or at any rate a portion of the Artillery, to move forward, it is all the more essential to provide this belt of Machine Gun fire as early as possible after the attacking troops have reached their final objective.

2. All necessary arrangements and calculations will be made beforehand (*see* Sec. 10, para 2).

Sec. 12.

3. These arrangements will contemplate the possibility of the attacking troops making good their final objective on one part of the front and failing to attain it on another. In order that the successful troops may not be compelled to withdraw, the protective barrage will have to be maintained ahead of them and at the same time drawn in to cover their exposed flank and the front of the troops who have advanced less far. This is only possible if and when the position of friendly troops is exactly known.

12.—UNITY OF METHOD IN ATTACK AND DEFENCE.

The method by which barrage fire is carried out is given in detail in Part II., and it is similar both for the attack and the defence, the only difference being that in defensive conditions the arrangements will on the whole be simpler. This unity of method is in accord with the fundamental unity between the offensive and defensive *rôles* of the Machine Gun. The attack, as already shown, implies the covering of an assault and the repulse of counter-attacks, and the defence, as will be shown in the sections which follow, develops an active nature in proportion as it is organized on scientific lines.

CHAPTER III.

WARFARE OF HIGHLY ORGANIZED DEFENCES—
THE DEFENSIVE.*

13.—PRINCIPLES OF DEFENCE.

1. The plan of defence in normal trench warfare legislates for an area organized in depth by one or more defensive systems.

2. The Front System is composed usually of an elaborate network of trenches and strong points, arranged roughly in three lines, as follows:—

(*a*) A First Line, which is in the nature of an observation or outpost line, and which as a general rule comprises a series of posts held by small numbers of Infantry with the help of Lewis Guns; these posts being connected by trenches.

(*b*) A Second or Support Line, which consists of a continuous line held in strength by the Infantry.

(*c*) A Reserve Line, generally the Main Line of Resistance, which consists of a connected series of strong points designed to:—

(i.) Break up an enemy attack by denying to him the most important features.

(ii.) Form rallying points behind which troops driven from the front two lines can be reformed.

(iii.) Split up an enemy attack in such a way that hostile elements which break through between the points shall be exposed to destruction in detail.

(iv.) Allow of counter-attacks issuing between them for the purpose of ejecting from the two first lines an enemy who has succeeded in establishing himself in them.

3. Behind this Front System will be other defended lines, or systems, consisting of woods and villages prepared for defence, and of trenches and redoubts commanding features of tactical importance.

---

* To be read in conjunction with S.S. 196 " Trench Warfare Diagrams for Infantry Officers."

4. The methods of employing Machine Guns for assisting in the defence of the Front System will alone be considered in this publication. All the principles of Machine Gun defence are contained therein, and the extent to which the Rear Systems can at any time be manned depends on the guns and personnel available.

5. The principle of economy of force is that as few men as possible shall be employed in a purely defensive *rôle*, whilst as many as possible are kept ready for offensive action.

This principle is observed when the fire power of Machine Guns is so employed that the trench system is held by a minimum of rifles and consequently with a minimum wastage of man power. (*See* Sec. 1, para. 4.)

6. The fullest service, however, cannot be rendered to Infantry Battalions unless there is close co-operation between the Artillery and Machine Guns. This point has already been noticed in Section 8 in connection with Harassing Fire previous to an attack. In defence it is of no less importance. The defence provided by the Artillery, Machine Guns and Trench Mortars must be a combined scheme in which the several arms supplement one another. In places where, and on occasions when, the number of Field Guns available precludes a complete defensive barrage of Artillery fire, co-ordination is all the more important.

7. In case of an enemy attack the *rôle* of the Machine Guns is:—

(*a*) To disorganize the attack in its origin by firing on the area from which it is launched.

(*b*) Should the enemy penetrate into the defended area, to arrest him by annihilating fire at short ranges, and hold him up at all costs until time has been gained for the preparation and launching of a counter-attack.

8. This *rôle* necessitates arrangements whereby effective belts of Machine Gun fire can be placed in the path of an advancing enemy.

The aim is not to site Machine Guns so that every yard of ground is swept by Machine Gun Fire, but so to combine the Machine Gun defence with that of the Lewis Guns of Infantry Battalions, that Machine Guns will play the part dictated by the characteristics of the weapon and will not be wasted in doing work which can be performed by Lewis Guns, such as firing on small depressions or down trenches. Machine Gun fire should be reserved for protection on a bigger scale, covering the more important features and denying to the enemy the most favourable routes of advance. Points of tactical importance must be strongly covered even though, owing to a shortage of guns, it is necessary to leave gaps on parts of the front where an enemy attack is improbable.

14.—TYPES OF MACHINE GUN FIRE.

Belts of Machine Gun Fire are of different types, according to the way they are produced:—

Type A.

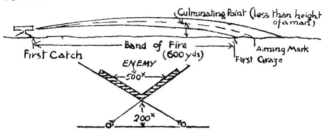

By bands of fire at short ranges where the culminating point is less than the height of a man. This kind of belt is especially suitable on flat ground, and it is very deadly; but, if used to cover the Front Line, it necessitates guns being placed well forward in the Front System.

Type B.

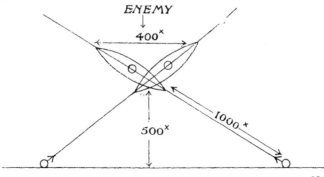

23

By oblique locking of beaten zones at moderate ranges.—
This type covers less ground per gun, but it allows of guns'
being placed further back. The extent of the zone varies with
the slope of the ground swept, being greater on ground falling
with respect to the line of sight.

Type C.

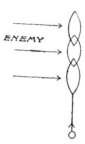

By locking in depth, that is to say, a flanking barrage.
This is a practical application of combined sights. It is most
suited for the protection of a salient or exposed flank, and
it may be possible to apply it to a re-entrant when the guns
themselves can be brought into a salient and fired almost
parallel to the front. The width of the beaten zone of a
Machine Gun being narrow, it may be advisable to duplicate
this belt where a high degree of protection is required.

Type D.

By frontal fire, in which the front covered by each gun depends on the number of guns available, but should not be more than 50 yards. The efficacy of this type of belt depends on : —

      (i.) The number of guns available and their rate of fire.

      (ii.) The angle of dive of the bullets (angle of dive = angle of descent for range, that is, angle of ground + angle of sight).

      (iii.) The time taken by hostile troops in passing through the belt.

This is the normal type of S.O.S. protective belt fired over the heads of the Infantry.

15.—DIRECT LAYING AND INDIRECT FIRE.

In comparing the scope for direct and indirect fire, it should be borne in mind that it is often possible to lay the guns by direct observation, and, subsequently, necessary to fire them indirect, either because the enemy's attack comes at night or early dawn, or because visibility is obscured by the smoke and dust of the enemy's bombardment and by his smoke screens. (*See* Sec. 5, para. 5.) Guns laid to fire direct should always be equipped for firing indirect, should the need arise.

16.—MUTUAL CO-OPERATION.

1. However numerous the guns employed, the defence will never possess the maximum power of resistance unless a complete plan of co-operation between the Machine Guns employed in a defended area is arranged.

2. This complete co-operation cannot be achieved unless the main plan of defence is laid down by the Corps for its whole front. This is necessary to secure : —

      (*a*) The linking-up of the defence on the flanks of neighbouring Corps and Divisions.

      (*b*) A continuity of policy. Divisions often stay only a short time in a particular sector ; and unless a continuous policy is adhered to, the system of defence is always in a state of flux and much time and labour are wasted.

3. Conversely, the execution of that part of the plan allotted to a Division must be a Divisional affair. This is necessary to ensure continuity of policy and proper co-operation between the Machine Gun Companies concerned.

4. Mutual Co-operation therefore implies : —

(*a*) A plan of defence which is outlined by the Corps and co-ordinated by the Division under its Divisional Machine Gun Commander. This secures central direction, the pooling of resources, and, as the result, the maximum of flexibility combined with the maximum of economy.

(*b*) A system that facilitates the use on a large scale of oblique fire. For example, an attack delivered in force on a narrow front may momentarily overwhelm the defences of a Brigade. Assistance should always be forthcoming from the Brigades on either flank, but this will rarely be obtained in time, unless it is arranged in advance in the Divisional plan.

Recent experience shows that co-operation on Divisional lines becomes imperative when the enemy launches a sudden offensive. It is therefore desirable to forestall this necessity by adopting, while conditions are normal, a scheme of Machine Gun defence which is flexible and amenable to control.

17.—CO-OPERATION WITH OTHER ARMS.

1. Divisional and Brigade Commanders must ensure that the plan of Machine Gun defence is in harmony with the distribution of the troops whom it is designed to protect, and Battalion Commanders must co-ordinate their Lewis Guns with this scheme and prevent overlapping or waste of fire power. There are cases where a Machine Gun can do rather more reliably the work which belongs to a Lewis Gun, but only at the expense of neglecting work which is essential to the general scheme of defence and which the Machine Gun alone can do.

2. Co-operation with the Artillery and Trench Mortars is required in order :—

(*a*) To work out a S.O.S. line of combined Artillery, Trench Mortar and Machine Gun fire in the proper proportions and of the desired depth.

(*b*) To co-operate in schemes of harassing fire at all times, and not merely on the eve of a big attack.

(*c*) To obtain information about the enemy, which the Artillery with its more elaborate system of observation has at its disposal.

3. Co-operation with the Engineers and Pioneer Companies is required in order:—

(*a*) That new wire may be sited in accordance with the plans of the Commander by representatives of the Machine Guns, Engineers and Infantry acting in concert. Machine Gun positions and wire should be sited simultaneously.

(*b*) That emplacements may be of the type required under the latest conditions, especially with regard to camouflage and tunnelling.

18.—METHOD OF HOLDING THE FRONT SYSTEM.
(*See* Sec. 13, para. 2.)

A sector of trenches should not be regarded as a mere series of successive defence lines to be held one after another, but as a single defended area the protection of which is laid out upon a definite plan, according to the nature of the ground.

The first question to consider in drawing up a plan of Machine Gun Defence for any sector of trenches is the Main Line of Resistance; that is, the line beyond which the enemy's attack must not penetrate. A decision on this point will decide the correct allotment of guns in depth.

It is possible for an intensive Artillery bombardment to destroy the Front and Support Lines, including any Machine Guns that may be in them, unless they are accommodated in deep dug-outs. If guns are kept in deep dug-outs in front trenches their chances of coming into action are small, since by the time they are mounted the enemy will be on top of them.

Machine Guns therefore will usually be placed in rear of the Support Line. The responsibility of holding the Front Line rests with Infantry Battalions and their Lewis Guns, assisted from the rear by Machine Guns.

19.—NUMBER OF GUNS IN FRONT SYSTEM.

The number of guns employed in the Front System will be determined by:—

(*a*) The total number of guns available.

(*b*) The nature of the ground and the tactical situation.

(*c*) The amount of cover that can be provided and the time that it will take to bring the guns into action.

(*d*) The arrangements for the relief of gun teams. These must be adequate and are especially important when heavy shelling, bad accommodation and severe weather have to be faced.

27

20.—CLASSES OF GUNS.

In conformity with the principle of defence in depth, provision must be made for a combination of direct and indirect fire; and, as in the offensive, the Machine Guns will fall naturally into two categories:—

      (*a*) Forward Guns. (*See* Sec. 4.)

      (*b*) Rear Guns. (*See* Sec. 5.)

21.—FORWARD GUNS.

1. These guns should, where possible, be arranged in pairs, each pair under the command of an Officer, or Sergeant. Each gun must have a N.C.O. as Gun Commander.

2. They should usually be placed in rear of the Second or Support Line, and between it and the Reserve Line.

3. They should be able to fire either by direct or indirect fire:—

      (*a*) On to No Man's Land, bringing oblique or flanking fire in front of the posts which constitute our Front Line. This is usually achieved by laying the lines of fire so that they pass between the posts and cross in front of them; *i.e.*, by the locking of Beaten Zones, as described in Sec. 14, Type B.

      (*b*) On the ground between the Front and Support Lines, putting Bands of Fire across it, as described in Sec. 14, Type A.

22.—GUNS IN OR NEAR THE FRONT LINE.

As stated in Sec. 21, para. 2, the Forward Guns should not normally be placed in front of the Support Line.

In exceptional cases, however, it may be desirable to place one or more Forward Guns in or near the Front Line, *e.g.*, where they can be defiladed from the enemy by rising ground, and are able from this vantage point to bring fire on important roads or trench junctions further down the line.

In all cases where guns are in or near the Front Line they must have local protection against surprise. A party of bombers and riflemen should always be at hand, and a bombing post established to prevent approach within bombing range of the gun positions. As Machine Gunners are trained to throw bombs, they should be provided with a small stock for use in an emergency.

23.—REAR GUNS.

1.   These guns will usually be placed in the neighbourhood and in rear of the Reserve Line or Main Line of Resistance.

2.   The ideal programme for these guns would be:—

(*a*) To provide a complete S.O.S. barrage line along the whole front; this line to be normally beyond the Artillery barrage line.

(*b*) In the event of a hostile penetration beyond the Support Line, to place Bands of Fire across the front of the strong points in the Reserve Line. These bands should be so arranged that the fire comes between the strong points and crosses in front of them. Where the number of guns does not permit the first part of the programme to be carried out completely, arrangements should be made in conjunction with the Artillery (*see* Sec. 17, para. 3), to put the S.O.S. barrage on selected parts of the front.

3.   The Rear Guns will usually be the guns employed for covering raids and other special enterprises. They will constitute a mobile reserve which will be in readiness to cope with emergencies on a particular part of the Divisional front or on the front of the Divisions on either flank. The fact that they are not involved in the close defence of the Front Line will facilitate conference with the Artillery and their detachment for special tasks.

24.—NIGHT FIRING BY FORWARD AND REAR GUNS.

1.   In normal times the bulk of Machine Gun firing will be done at night. The execution of night firing must never be allowed to become a mechanical and perfunctory performance. In this work it is possible, even when the general situation is quiet, to maintain the offensive spirit.

2.   The targets must be well selected and the volume of fire sufficient. The requisite intensity of fire should be obtained by increasing the number of Machine Guns rather than by allotting bigger tasks to a restricted number. Both classes of· guns, therefore, forward and barrage, will be employed.

3.   Each night's firing should be part of a programme, which is based on the information obtained by the Divisional Machine Gun Commander from the latest intelligence and the night firing programme of the Artillery.

4. Provided that an alternative position is available in case of need, it will usually be safe, and always more convenient, for guns which have well equipped S.O.S. positions concealed from view to do their night firing from these. But guns whose S.O.S. position is exposed or very close to the Front Line must move elsewhere for night work. This night position must allow of fire on the S.O.S. Line.

5. The difference between normal night firing and the harassing fire carried out mainly at night time prior to a " set-piece " attack (*see* Sec. 8) is merely one of degree. The methods and organization are identical.

25.—DEFENCE IN DEPTH AND THE " OFFENSIVE " DEFENCE.

An observance of the principles laid down will result in a zone of Machine Gun defences organized in depth rather than a series of positions covering, and limited to, successive trench lines. The object of placing Machine Guns in depth is to secure fire in depth from the enemy's front system back to our own reserve lines; but the guns themselves should not be dotted indiscriminately over the zone, as they will then not be easy to control, and the organization therefore not flexible. Control and flexibility are essential to the " offensive " defence mentioned in Sec. 23, para. 3, and Sec. 24 above. For this kind of work and the " set-piece " offensive itself the Machine Guns must always be prepared. A system of passive defence is destructive of efficiency, and, furthermore, overlooks the important function of inspiring the troops with confidence.

26.—FIRE CONTROL OF THE FORWARD GUNS.
(*See* Section 21.)

1. Direct observation of the situation from the gun position and fire on previously arranged S.O.S. lines will, as a rule, be the only methods of control possible once the enemy attack has commenced.

2. In order that the guns may be able to fire as directed in Sec. 21, para. 3, there will be two prescribed lines of fire, of which the first will bring them on to No Man's Land as described in Sec. 21, 3 (*a*), while they can be switched without delay on to the second as described in Sec. 21, 3 (*b*). Fire will be opened on the latter, as soon as it is ascertained that the

enemy has penetrated beyond the First Line into the vicinity of the Support Line, and the situation as regards our own troops is sufficiently clear.

Until then fire will be maintained on the S.O.S. line, and the barrage thus formed, combined with that of the Rear Machine Guns, Artillery and Trench Mortars, should prevent the enemy being reinforced, and enable the Infantry Battalions to deal with those of the enemy's troops which have succeeded in entering the front position.

3. Precise instructions must be issued as to the fire of these Forward Guns, and their action and lines of fire in case of an attack explained in advance to the Infantry Battalions concerned.

4. In an entrenched position, the ability to repulse the enemy does not depend on the number of men in the trenches before the bombardment begins, but on the amount of fire that can be delivered against the enemy when his barrage lifts and his Infantry advances. If the trenches are thickly manned:—

(a) Heavy loss is caused by the bombardment.

(b) Difficulty is experienced by the Forward Machine Guns in bringing fire to bear on the enemy without hitting their own troops.

5. These disadvantages are reduced to a minimum, when the First and Support Lines are held lightly and arrangements exist whereby certain portions of the trench system in, and in front of, the Second Line are marked as being in the danger zone of Machine Gun fire from the moment the S.O.S. Signal goes up, as well as later when the Machine Guns are firing on their second lines of fire in the manner just described.

The routes which will be used for movement between the Front and Support Lines should be definitely laid down and known by the Machine Gunners.

Arrangements of this nature will enable the full power of the Machine Gun to be developed from the beginning of the attack and maintained throughout. Large areas of ground will be denied to the enemy, his attack will be kept "below ground," that is to say, confined to working up the trenches themselves, and the task left to Infantry Battalions of dealing with those of the enemy who have penetrated beyond the Front Line will be facilitated.

6. Thus, by careful arrangements, precise instructions and a thorough understanding between Infantry Battalions and Machine Gunners, it will be possible to ensure that confusion, delay in opening fire and risk to our own troops from the fire of Machine Guns are minimised, and Battalions will be able to rely on obtaining support from the Machine Guns from the outset of the enemy attack.

27.—FIRE CONTROL OF THE REAR GUNS.

In a similar manner the Rear Guns will primarily have two lines of fire:—

(*a*) On their S.O.S. line.

(*b*) On their close defence line.

Fire will be maintained on the S.O.S. Line until it becomes evident that, owing to the advance made by the enemy, fire at close ranges is necessary in order to protect the Reserve Line.

Fire on the S.O.S. Line, in conjunction with that of the Artillery and Trench Mortars, should prevent the enemy being reinforced, and thus enable the Infantry garrison and Forward Machine Guns to deal effectively with those enemy troops who may have succeeded in penetrating the front position.

28.—S.O.S. SIGNAL.

It will rarely be possible for the Rear Guns to have their fire controlled by direct observation from the vicinity of the gun position. Communication by runner is obviously out of the question, being far too slow for S.O.S. purposes. Visual signalling and telephonic communications are the only alternatives. The normal method of signalling an attack is the sending up by the Infantry of a S.O.S. Signal. This is effective provided it is observed, but it is a common experience that the S.O.S. Signal is either missed or misunderstood. The Machine Guns cannot afford to wait until they hear the Artillery opening up; for it is the *rôle* of the Rear Machine Guns to open fire on their S.O.S. Line the moment the attack is signalled, and, if possible, before the enemy have reached our wire. The greatest value of these guns is during the first two minutes of an attack, and they must aim to get their fire down even more speedily than the Artillery, and even before the Very lights have burnt out.

It is therefore necessary that all Machine Gunners should know what the Signal is, from where it will be fired, and in what direction. Picking up the S.O.S. Signal should be frequently rehearsed both on Field Ranges and in the line. If there is any risk that the S.O.S. Signal will not be picked up by the Rear Guns, a Forward Observation Officer, connected with these by telephone, should be stationed in front. There are numerous examples of the successful results of such an arrangement.

29.—TELEPHONIC COMMUNICATION.

1. No proper system of Fire Control is possible without telephonic communication. This is indispensable between :—

(*a*) Forward Observation Posts and :—

(i.) O.C. Machine Guns in the Brigade Area.

(ii.) Rear Guns.

(iii.) Report Centres of Forward Guns.

(*b*) O.C. Machine Guns in the Brigade Area and :—

(i.) Rear Guns.

(ii.) Report Centres of Forward Guns.

(*c*) Divisional Machine Gun Commander and O.C. Machine Guns in the several Brigade Areas.

2. In addition, every effort should be made to link up by telephone, pairs of Forward Guns with their Report Centres, of which there should be two or more in each Brigade Area connected up with the Forward Observation Post and the O.C. Machine Guns in the manner just described.

Wherever possible telephone communication must be duplicated by visual signalling.

The Report Centre will usually be a Battalion Headquarters (*see* Sec. 4, para. 12), and, therefore, when separate lines are not available, it should be possible to arrange that the Forward Guns can send and receive messages from the Headquarters of the nearest Infantry Company over the Battalion line.

3. Communication with the rear *viâ* the Divisional Machine Gun Commander puts the guns in immediate touch with information from the Artillery, the Royal Flying Corps and adjacent Divisions.

4. It is only by the above means that it will be possible to make the Machine Gun defence flexible, rapid in execution, and of the greatest value to Infantry Battalions.

30.—THE BATTERY SYSTEM.

1. The Battery System, *i.e.*, a group of guns usually eight in number under the control of a Battery Commander, is an established feature of barrage work in offensive operations. The system can be applied to the defensive barrage. It is possible that here a battery of four guns, which is less easy of detection, may be a large enough unit in normal conditions, but the better the communications the more elastic the Battery system can become, without sacrificing its fundamental characteristic—unity of control.

2. An arrangement of the Main Line Defence on the Battery principle has these advantages:—

(*a*) It suits the principle of defence in depth.

(*b*) It saves much time which is otherwise spent in the tour and inspection of isolated gun positions.

(*c*) It reduces to a minimum the difficulties of ammunition supply.

(*d*) It makes the system of defence more flexible. The Rear Guns will be available for other work than fire on a single S.O.S. Line. Their fire can be switched on to new danger zones, in response to calls from the Divisional Machine Gun Commander, Forward Observation Officer and Infantry Commanders. The speedy response of the concentrated fire of many guns is the most telling fashion in which the surprise effect of Machine Guns can in existing conditions be attained.

(*e*) It makes the Machine Guns a better instrument for co-operation with the Artillery in the " offensive " defence.

3. A combination consisting of the minimum of Forward Guns, consistent with their being able to perform the duties already outlined, and of Rear Guns organized on the Battery system, will be found a good working combination under most circumstances, especially when the defence is that of newly won ground, where little or no protection for Forward Guns exists.

31.—SNIPING BATTERIES.

A Battery connected by telephone with a forward observation station can be employed as a Sniping Battery. By the aid of his Fighting Map (*see* Part II.) the Forward Observation Officer is able to send down the necessary fire orders in a simple form in the minimum of time. On many parts of the front visible targets are rare, but after a successful offensive they are often numerous, and where Sniping Batteries have been employed on the principles laid down in this publication they have obtained good results.

Trained observation is indispensable. The observer who is conversant with the principles of the enemy's scheme of defence (*see* Sec. 39), will be able to locate targets from momentary glimpses and casual hints which would be lost on the uninformed observer, however keen his eyesight.

The reporting of targets, and of fire effect (when this can be observed), gives confidence to the Machine Gun personnel, and at a minimum cost in material stops overland movement by day within Machine Gun range.

32.—SITING OF MACHINE GUNS.

1. Guns must be sited with reference to the *rôle* they have to play in the plan of defence. One of the disadvantages of putting guns in the vicinity of the Front Line is that the gun position is subject to continuous enemy annoyance and supervision, and to complete destruction in case of an intense enemy bombardment. The position is, therefore, likely to be weak tactically and materially. A site, well in rear of the Front Line, can be selected in the strongest tactical position, and the strong points or trench lines can be planned to conform to the lines of fire of the Machine Guns.

2. In general, owing to the concentrated Artillery fire which is likely to be directed on it, positions in any clearly defined trench system should be avoided. Aerial observation, however, makes the concealment of positions in the open increasingly difficult. Such a position should not be surrounded by belts of high wire, which indicate its presence to the airman. During the process of construction, the excavation and building materials should be carefully camouflaged. Even though all movement takes place at night, tracks may be made which show up on photographs. It is, therefore, often advisable to select a site near a piece of trench system and use this as an avenue of approach. The track from the trench to the position can then be continued past the position to a trench beyond it, and made to resemble a new short cut in the existing trench system.

3. Mobility, alternative positions, and frequent changes of location are, along with camouflage, the best ways of ensuring concealment. The further the guns are from the

Front Line, the less the difficulties of moving. A change of location will be imperative for a Battery of guns, if there are clear indications that they have been spotted.

4. Wire entanglements should be arranged so as to force the enemy in a particular direction, which will bring him into a belt of Machine Gun fire.

It is not advisable to place Machine Guns in the angle of the wire, where the enemy is bound to suspect their presence. Only dummy emplacements should be constructed at these points, the actual Machine Gun èmplacements being sited in concealed ground to a flank or in rear.

In the laying out of new Field Works and new wire, close co-operation between the Engineers and the Machine Gun Corps is essential. (*See* Sec. 17, para. 3; and Sec. 36, para. 5.)

6. (*a*) The slope of the ground is an important consideration in the siting of Machine Guns; and for the Machine Gunners the choice of slope will usually be wide when the scheme of defence is in depth and the ground is surveyed from the standpoint of the Division and Corps.

(*b*) A forward slope offers the big advantage of direct laying and continuous observation of the movements of troops, in case the guns have to change from long range indirect fire to direct fire across their immediate front. The serious drawback is the risk of detection from enemy observation posts or balloons, and the difficulty of moving while under observation. Where the position on the forward slope can be ingeniously concealed, it may, by its inherent improbability, escape artillery fire.

(*c*) A reverse slope now presents no serious drawback to overhead fire. Its advantage is that it allows of unobserved movement up to the position. When guns are in a Battery, it also conceals the unavoidable traffic between gun and gun, but because of its natural advantages it is likely to be marked down by the enemy's artillery, and (if it is an isolated feature) to be subjected to a concentration of fire.

(*d*) The ideal slope is, perhaps, one defiladed from the front and sloping obliquely to the enemy. This kind of slope is more likely to offer itself in hilly country with spurs and intersecting valleys. The guns can then be sited so that they flank any attempt to cross the valley and, with frontal fire, prevent the enemy ascending it. Care must be taken in these cases that the tops of the ridges are commanded by guns placed in other positions.

33.—TYPES OF EMPLACEMENT.

1. The type of emplacement selected will be governed by the *rôle* of the gun, the lie of the ground, the labour available, the nature of the soil and the proximity of the enemy.

2. *Covered Loophole Emplacements.*—These, when built into a clearly defined trench system (as contrasted with strongholds in woods and industrial areas), are seldom suitable nowadays. Even strong concrete will not stand a modern bombardment, and the loophole faces get knocked about or blocked up or masked by shell debris. In sandy ground there is an additional drawback: unless the floor of the loophole emplacement is made of solid material and kept swept of sand hourly, the draught, when the loophole screen is lowered, drives a cloud of sand on to the gun and into the firer's face. Furthermore, the cordite fumes from certain marks of S.A.A. are injurious to the gun numbers confined in such an emplacement, and will necessitate the wearing of respirators during firing. On the other hand, firing under cover, in addition to reducing minor casualties, increases the gunner's confidence.

Covered emplacements will often be found suitable:—

(*a*) In naturally protected places such as woods, houses and mine buildings.

(*b*) In battery positions, when these are sited on reverse slopes, from which the work of construction will not be visible to the enemy. In this case there will be no loopholes. (*See* diagram in Appendix II.)

3. *Open emplacements*, connected by covered way or open trench, with neighbouring emplacements and a central dug-out.

The advantage of this type is that it is easily constructed, so that numerous alternative positions can be prepared in advance. In Battery positions the open emplacement facilitates fire control, setting out of aiming posts, and laying off from reference objects. If, however, the central dug-out is any distance from the emplacements, there is a danger that the team will never reach them under a bombardment.

The most modern form of open emplacement is the adapted shell hole, or series of shell-holes, which from its resemblance to the surrounding terrain is difficult to detect.

4. *Emplacements of the Champagne Type.*—The plan is a double shaft leading up from a dug-out between the two. One shaft is the entrance, and from the other shaft the gun is fired.

37

There is, therefore, no distance between the dug-out and the gun position. The firing shaft opens out into a shell-hole, or bit of natural cover, or on to a carefully camouflaged slit in the ground. In isolated positions, or positions covering strong points, this is generally the best type of emplacement.

A strong tunnelled system leading out to inconspicuous emplacements, which are little more than stances for the gun, combines many of the advantages of covered and open emplacements. Weak tunnels, however, are only traps.

34.—EQUIPMENT OF GUN POSITIONS.

1. Whether in actual occupation or not, all gun positions, other than alternative positions, should be equiped with the following:—

(i.) Order Board.   } *See* Appendix I.
(ii.) List of Stores.   }
(iii.) Fighting Map.

Occupied positions only:—
Intelligence Summary.

2. The Fighting Maps should show the Zero line, line of fire for S.O.S., line of fire for close defence, and the lines of fire of the guns on either flank.

The Intelligence Summary should contain:—

(i.) The calculations from which the Fighting Map has been made.

(ii.) List of targets (with calculations) for harassing fire.

(iii.) A record of all fighting done and the targets engaged.

(iv.) Notes on the ground visible from the gun position.

(v.) Position of Section Officer's Dug-out, and the Machine Gun Company Headquarters.

(vi.) Information as to relief routes, dumps, etc.

3. Wherever possible gun positions should be provided with a shelter for belt filling and gun cleaning, and also with a dug-out for the gun team. Recesses should be constructed in which to keep the gun, spare parts, and belt boxes. One of these recesses should be made gas proof, and at least half the belt boxes at the gun kept in it.

CHAPTER IV.

35.—ATTACK AND DEFENCE OF WOODED AREAS AND TOWNS.

1. *Wooded Areas.*—Large wooded areas will be the scene of highly organized resistance, owing to the fact that they lend themselves to defence by nests of Machine Guns, distributed in depth. The attacking troops can be diverted by well arranged obstacles, natural and artificial (thickets, wire, palissades, and the like), on to paths or clearings which are swept by the fire of concealed Machine Guns. Even when the gun has been located, it will be hard to silence, for it will be in a strong position, fortified with loopholes and overhead protection, which is denied to Artillery observation by the surrounding undergrowth and foliage.

If such an area has to be attacked, it can only be reduced by the systematic process of a piecemeal bombardment. Its reduction will be of necessity very slow, and the individual Machine Gun will not be handicapped by its environment. The Artillery can only single out for special concentration a particular part of a forest, in the sense that they can single out a particular map square in any area of similar dimensions.

2. *Towns and Industrial Areas.*—(a) Such areas cannot be passed by or easily enveloped like a small village. Envelopment will usually be the aim of the attacking force, but when the process involves a Corps or a whole Army, the Brigades and Divisions in the heart of it will be compelled to fight for the ground in detail and incorporate the pieces, as they are won, into a scheme of suburban defences.

(b) To erect a protective belt either by direct bands of fire or obliquely locked zones (*see* Sec. 14), is a difficult thing in a maze of half-demolished buildings; but a big town, with a central area and suburbs and streets leading out to these across a waste of fields, railway sidings, reservoirs, slag heaps, and the like, offers exceptional opportunities for a defensive flanking barrage.

(c) The same holds good for the attack. Such a district is reduced irregularly in the process of envelopment. Unusual salients are created by the artificial features on the ground. It is, therefore, generally possible to obtain positions from which the streets, in whatever direction they run, can be caught in enfilade.

(*d*) A " set-piece " attack will therefore tend to take the following form:—Whilst the Heavy Artillery bombards the mine heads (Fosses, Puits, etc.), public buildings, chateaux, and street rows, the Machine Guns will supplement the barrage of the Field Artillery by placing a flanking barrage along slag heaps, avenues and streets. The occupants of the houses, if they try to run away, will (in the absence of underground communications) either be caught by Machine Gun fire, or confined to the tedious and dangerous course of working from ruin to ruin. All traffic junctions within range and strike of the bullet (the two things are by no means identical) will be similarly swept.

(*e*) Frontal fire on roofs and walls is very demoralising to the occupants. It will, therefore, be advisable to combine frontal with enfilade fire.

As this kind of frontal fire is mainly for moral effect, each gun can be given a bigger frontage than usual, and this will free more guns for the enfilade of different streets.

(*f*) A rain of harassing fire at night, planned on the same principles, and incessantly maintained, will greatly lower the spirit of the defence.

(*g*) When Machine Guns are placed among buildings, Reference Objects are usually very hard to find. Often nothing can be seen from the position except the immediate field of fire, so that the gun must be laid for indirect fire by compass.

(*h*) As a site for Machine Guns, a house is to be avoided if it is isolated or if it abuts on cross roads, but when it forms part of a group it offers certain advantages:—

> (i.) The cellars make dry and comfortable dugouts; and when they have been in enemy occupation, many will already have been strengthened. In this case, however, precautions must be taken against traps and land mines. The ventilation holes facing the enemy must be strongly covered; and, when captured buildings are first entered, it must be remembered that it is the enemy's custom to block up the front windows and leave gaps or open windows in the rear, through which the light of a match or torch will be detected.

(ii.) Provided that, it has been strutted (which usually is feasible owing to the abundance of mine props and derelict wood-work), the basement of a house will sometimes withstand a direct hit on the house itself. In that case the growing pile of bricks adds to the strength of the cellars beneath.*

(iii.) Cellar windows afford natural loopholes in abundance, and require little or no external work before use as a Machine Gun emplacement. If they become masked by shell debris it is usually possible to find an alternative position outside without much difficulty. Whether the emplacement is inside or outside the cellar, care will have to be taken that the gun and ammunition boxes are kept clear of brick dust, which, mixing with the oil, forms a paste that clogs the working parts of the gun.

(iv.) Where the upper storeys are standing, they are useful as observation posts; and on occasions Machine Guns can be fired from them. Instances have occurred in which Machine Guns so placed have covered the advance of Infantry with direct overhead fire, sweeping the top of the Fosse or other point, which was the Infantry's objective.

---

* The enemy makes a practice of building concrete emplacements in a ground floor room, and firing his Machine Guns through the window or a hole. These emplacements are a room within a room, and apparently capable of withstanding the heaviest shelling.

CHAPTER V.

36.—ORGANIZATION OF DEFENCE OF CAPTURED POSITIONS.

1. The principles of organizing in depth the defence of ground won are identical with those that govern the placing of Machine Guns in a system of highly organized defences.

2. The Forward Guns, whose *rôle* during the offensive has been detailed in Sec. 4, will be sited with a view to carrying out the same duties in defence. As they move up to their selected positions in the manner already described (Sec. 4, paras. 5-9), these guns, in conjunction with the Rear Guns following on behind, will at no stage violate the principle of a distribution in depth, and from the outset of their location in a new environment will assume naturally a *rôle* similar to that which they discharged in the settled warfare of the trenches.

3. In the plan drafted before the opening of the offensive operation, the problem of disposing Machine Guns in depth will need to be considered as a whole, and the disposition taken will conform to the arrangements then made.

4. These arrangements will contemplate a scheme of defence of the same order as before (*see* Sec. 13), namely :—

(*a*) A series of defended shell-holes, etc., not forming a continuous line, corresponding to the First Line in ordinary trench warfare.

(*b*) A line of supporting points, corresponding to the Support Line, and occupied in greater depth.

(*c*) A line of defended localities, or converted enemy entrenchments, corresponding to the Reserve Line.

5. The reconnaissance for the Forward Guns should be made in conjunction with the reconnoitring detachment of Engineers, which follows in the wake of the attacking Infantry. When the gun teams reach their destination, their function will be two-fold :—

(i.) To cover Infantry and Working Parties of Pioneers who are engaged on the construction of strong points and lines of resistance.

(ii.) To co-operate with the Engineers in laying
out Machine Gun fields of fire and constructing
Machine Gun emplacements, the object being to secure
a sequence of work, in which, as the initial stage,
Machine Gun fields of fire are selected with reference
to the possibilities of the ground, and themselves
determine the conformation of the wire which the
Engineers are proceeding to lay.

When the organization of the defence is sufficiently
advanced, the guns will, where necessary, move from the
positions temporarily taken up in the course of the battle
to those allotted to them in the newly constructed system
in accordance with the plans of the Commander (*see* Section
17, para. 3).

6. The Forward Guns will be located normally between
the Support and Reserve Lines. As in the defence of highly
organized positions, they will have two lines of fire:—

(*a*) Between the advanced posts of the Front Line
on to the ground in front, which they will protect
with a belt of Type " B " (as described in Sec. 14
and Sec. 21, para. 3).

(*b*) Along the ground in front of the Support
Line, which they will protect with bands of short range
fire.

As the advanced posts do not form a continuous line, their
power of resistance will be strengthened, without risk to the
occupants, by Machine Guns firing between them from the
rear.

7. The forward movement of the Rear Guns (*see* Sec.
10), demands judicious timing and foresight.

(*a*) From the nature of their employment they
cannot cross No Man's Land before the enemy barrage
comes down. Some time after Zero, they must pass
through this barrage, thick or thin. Therefore, as
much latitude as possible should be allowed to them
as regards the moment at which they will move
forward.

(*b*) The fire of the Rear Guns at their intermediate positions is an essential part of the battle
action, and either from there, or from their final positions, they will nearly always be called upon for a
S.O.S. barrage. Every effort should therefore be made

to avoid selecting positions on the enemy's barrage line. The fact that the enemy will naturally select for his barrage distinctive lines like a support trench, a road or a river, must be set against the temptation to send the Rear Guns to these easily recognisable features. If the Rear Guns have the misfortune to strike the barrage line, their fire may be neutralized, and they may be forced to move elsewhere. This will involve the working out of new calculations, which is a difficult matter in the stress of an action, even for a highly trained personnel.

(*c*) The Divisional Machine Gun Commander must carefully lay down beforehand the organization of the Rear Guns after an attack. Even when the Battery System is maintained as a normal part of the defensive structure, certain modifications in detail (re-grouping, thinning out of Batteries, etc.) will usually be necessary.

(*d*) Owing to the strain, physical and nervous, which is imposed on a team that has first of all to fire a timed barrage, and subsequently to keep on the alert for S.O.S. calls, their relief should not be delayed, preparations having been made for this in advance in accordance with Sec. 6, para. 3. When fresh Divisions take over the new line, they will be apt to press for the retention of the old personnel, who are familiar with the situation. But all experience is against the policy of keeping the same teams in the same barrage positions longer than is absolutely necessary after the attack.

(*e*) The plan of defence will be completed by the final location of the Rear Guns in rear of the new Reserve Line. There they will resume a defensive *rôle*, two-fold in nature, corresponding to that which they occupied before the advance. (*See* Sec. 23, para. 2.)

CHAPTER VI.

WARFARE OF IMPROVISED DEFENCES AND OPEN FIGHTING.

37.—SPECIAL CONSIDERATIONS.

1. Important as are the organization and arrangement of the work of Machine Guns in warfare against highly organized defences, they are even more important after the main defended area has been broken through, and the fighting has resolved itself into the attack and defence of more or less hastily organized defences.

2. The more open the fighting becomes, the more will troops get away from the " mass " of their artillery and have to depend on Machine Guns to do some portion of the work for which they have been accustomed to rely on the Artillery.

It is precisely in places where such a situation arises that a working scheme between the Artillery, Machine Guns, and Trench Mortars will enable a division of* labour to be arranged, in which, by taking on definite tasks, such as the neutralization of certain areas, the Machine Guns will be able to do some of the Artillery work, and thereby enable the Artillery to concentrate more guns for other and perhaps more important purposes.

3. The more open the fighting, the more effective is the Machine Gun, and the more self-reliance and judgment are required to apply the principles laid down in this publication: and if (to take an extreme case) the Artillery were entirely eliminated, the Machine Gun would be called upon to provide the principal neutralizing and covering fire.

In trench warfare the Artillery is the principal protection of the Infantry against enemy Machine Guns. While the enemy are in occupation of a highly organized defensive area, which has been under close observation for a long period, it is more difficult for the enemy to conceal the position of his Machine Guns, and, therefore, easier for the Artillery to destroy them, or at any rate neutralize their fire.

But in more open conditions of fighting it will be much harder for the Artillery to locate and deal with them.

Furthermore, whenever the enemy resistance is stout, the advance must be preceded and supported by some form of covering fire. Open warfare implies movement. The Machine Gun is more mobile than the Field Gun, and it is the only weapon outside the Artillery which is capable of covering an attack by sustained long range overhead fire.

4. Care must be taken to ensure that in the confusing circumstances of a considerable forward movement, the fire power of the Machine Guns is not misapplied or wasted. Machine Guns at once lose the greater part of their value if they are hurried forward from their limbers, with inadequate supplies of ammunition, into positions where their fire is masked by Lewis Guns and Infantry outposts. The comparative mobility of the Machine Guns does not mean that their teams on foot can keep pace with a Battalion. Similarly, though Machine Guns on pack animals can go wherever a horse can go, when removed from pack animals they are less mobile than Cavalry units.

The definite attachment of Machine Guns to Infantry Battalions (*see* Sec. 4, para. 2) generally defeats its own end. Machine Guns, if they are kept well in hand, are at once an instrument of offence and a reserve of fire power within reach of the Infantry Commander; but, if they are involved in the details of a Battalion's movements, full use cannot be made of them.

5. The situation which has to be foreseen is one in which little or no Artillery is for the moment available. Machine Guns will be called upon, and, if properly handled, should be able to assist in making good the shortage of Artillery. Apart from their obvious value for strengthening the covering fire, the effective use of Machine Guns for neutralizing strong points, nests of Machine Guns, and even the Field Battery positions of the enemy—tasks which in the conditions of warfare hitherto prevailing have been relegated almost entirely to the Artillery—may make the whole difference between the success or failure of operations in which the available Artillery support is necessarily limited.

6. This, however, pre-supposes :—

(*a*) A high standard of training and technical ability on the part of Machine Gunners.

(*b*) The allotment of suitable tasks in advance and careful arrangements to that end.

(*c*) The closest co-operation with the Artillery.

Co-operation with the Artillery in trench warfare, and in the preparation for and execution of " set piece " offensives, is the best guarantee that these *desiderata* will be forthcoming later.

38.—GENERAL PRINCIPLES.

1. The general principles for the employment of Machine Guns are the same, whether the warfare be that of highly organized defences, or warfare of a more open nature. While the enemy is himself on the move, the fire power of Machine Guns must be used to endeavour to prevent him settling down, but once he has taken up a defensive position, a "set-piece" attack has usually to be organized, and then, however small the attack may be, the work of the available Machine Guns must be prepared in exactly the same manner as has already been described.

2.. However open the warfare may become, the organization of the Machine Guns still falls naturally into two distinct categories:—

(*a*) The guns pushed forward to support closely the Infantry Battalions and corresponding to the Forward Guns, whose duties have been described in Secs. 4 and 36.

(*b*) The guns retained for special covering fire, either direct or indirect, and corresponding to the Rear Guns. (*See* Secs. 5 and 36.)

3. (*a*) If the Machine Guns are to be of real assistance to the attacking troops when the available 18-pdr. support is limited, a high percentage of the total guns must be detailed for the duty mentioned in para. 2 (*b*) above.

Otherwise it will be impossible to re-concentrate the Machine Guns for overhead covering fire, either for assisting the Infantry advance, or resisting counter-attacks against positions already gained.

(*b*) The Machine Guns allotted under para. 2 (*b*) above should:—

(i.) Be organized in Mobile Batteries of 4, 6, or 8 guns each, as convenient.

(ii.) Advance by bounds and be allotted definite halting places at the end of each bound.

(iii.) Keep in close touch with the advancing Infantry, so as to be able to move up quickly and come into action when and where required.

(*c*) Each Group of Mobile Batteries should be under the command of an officer detailed as Group Commander.

This officer must make a careful study of the ground on his probable route of advance, consider the various positions from which he may be called upon to use his Batteries, and have his Headquarters at the Headquarters of the Brigade whose advance he is covering.

(*d*) In the event of a complete initial success, formations pushing forward early beyond the range of adequate Field Artillery support should be allotted a large proportion of the available Mobile Batteries in order that the shortage of Field Artillery may in some measure be made good.

(*e*) Machine Guns pushed forward " amongst " the Infantry are seldom able to render actual support during an advance, and are mainly of use for the defence of the ground won. These guns should therefore : —

> (i.) Be only a small proportion of the total number available.
>
> (ii.) Usually work in sub-sections.
>
> (iii.) Advance by bounds along a definite line of advance.
>
> (iv.) Be allotted definite halting places at the end of each bound.

(*f*) The organization of a large proportion of the available Machine Guns into Mobile Batteries, has, in addition to its power of offensive action by supporting the Infantry advance, the great advantage of : —

> (i.) Forming a strong rear line of defence in case of a reverse.
>
> (ii.) Forming a reserve of fire power in the hand of the Commander, available to assist in exploiting a success.

(*g*) The question of the supply of an adequate amount of S.A.A. for the Mobile Batteries is necessarily a difficult one, and all arrangements for getting it forward and the forming of advanced dumps must be carefully worked out before the advance begins.

(*h*) For the organization of the defence the fire power of Machine Guns is best employed by having a small proportion of the available Machine Guns forward for defence *in depth* of the ground gained, and the remainder retained in their battery organization for the purpose of : —

> (i.) Putting down an S.O.S. barrage along the front of the position to be defended.
>
> (ii.) Concentrating their fire against a counter-attack, or on an area from which a counter-attack is being initiated.

(*i*) The placing of large numbers of Machine Guns actually *in* the position to be defended has proved itself to be wasteful in personnel and material, and not nearly so effective as the method outlined in (*h*) above.

(*j*) The Divisional Machine Gun Commander should not personally command a group of Machine Gun Batteries.

He should keep in close touch with his Divisional Headquarters, supervise generally the supply arrangements of the forward Batteries, and be in readiness to direct any reorganization necessary to meet a change of circumstances.

4. In regions where the enemy makes a voluntary retirement to conform with a retirement imposed on him elsewhere, we shall have to pass through, and perhaps remain on, a network of undestroyed fortifications. The Machine Guns will have to be placed either in these fortifications or in the vacant ground between them. In these circumstances the following considerations must be weighed : —

> (*a*) An old strong point may only have been a strong point because it contained guns and faced a certain way. It will be known to the enemy, and if it possesses no natural strength it should be avoided.

> (*b*) In winter especially, it will be of convenience to select positions near to existing dug-outs which are water proof and perhaps shell proof. The fact that prepared defences need a minimum of new work is an argument in their favour.

5. In organized defences the task of silencing enemy Machine Guns belongs primarily to the Artillery, but among improvised defences Machine Guns will be capable of taking a bigger share in this. Lewis Guns, owing to their greater mobility, will be more successful in stalking single Machine Guns at close quarters, but Machine Guns should be effective in silencing by concentrated fire active enemy nests.

6. In warfare of an open nature there will be full scope for the bold handling of Machine Guns, but boldness does not mean unnecessary exposure to Artillery fire or snipers.

7. Machine Guns will in most cases be sufficiently protected by the dispositions of the troops with whom they are acting. Where the Machine Gun Commander finds himself in an exposed position, he will take such steps as may be necessary to guard his detachment against surprise.

8. The situation will sometimes arise in which the simultaneous delivery of two or more loosely connected attacks results in exposing the inner flanks of the attacking forces. Should an attack develop against a line of defended localities, it may happen that neighbouring troops are drawn apart towards the several centres of resistance, thus creating a gap through which the enemy can issue to deliver a counter attack on their flanks.

A battery of Machine Guns, placed so as to command the ground over which the counter attack is likely to come, will be able, owing to the great fire power which it can instantly develop, to nip in the bud any such enterprise on the part of the enemy. The method of controlling the fire of Machine Gun Batteries, described in Part II. of this publication, enables their fire to be directed rapidly on to a new target or threatened area.

39.—RECONNAISSANCE AND APPRECIATION OF THE TACTICAL SITUATION.

1. An accurate knowledge of the enemy's method of defence is desirable, inasmuch as the enemy is himself expert in Machine Gun defence, and takes the weight of our assault on a zone of defences cleverly studded with Machine Guns. Moreover, as territory is gradually wrested from him, it becomes necessary to incorporate into our own defended system, ground that has already been put in a state of defence by him. Machine Gun Officers should, therefore, study carefully the Intelligence Summaries and special publications in which the information on this subject, obtained from prisoners and captured orders, is reproduced.

2. This general knowledge must be supplemented by exact reconnaissance on the ground itself. A study of the map and, through glasses, of the ground in combination with the map must precede and follow the actual visit to the ground This will make the reconnaissance what it should be—the recognition of a situation already envisaged in the rough. The picture thus obtained should be checked, when occasion offers, by aerial photographs, and the map kept up to date by the insertion of new details extracted from the Intelligence Summaries. None of these aids, however, should be allowed to interfere with the examination of the actual ground.

In the isolated operations of more open warfare, Machine Gun Officers will have to collect for themselves much of the information which is supplied by Army Headquarters on the eve of a " set-piece " offensive. Only thus will it be possible to select in advance suitable localities for the guns and to detect places from which trouble is likely to occur.

It must be remembered that the unexpected will often occur, and can only be met correctly by an intelligent application of principles.

3. The approach to positions must be conducted on the same principle as the forward movement of the Forward Guns in a " set-piece " offensive : —

> (*a*) The guns will keep in sub-sections of two guns at least.

> (*b*) From the moment of leaving limbers they will advance by " bounds."

> (*c*) The line of advance for the guns and their halting place at each " bound " will be laid down.

> (*d*) A reconnoitring officer, covered by his scouts, will go forward to reconnoitre routes, and will order up the guns to selected localities, from which they can best assist the Infantry Battalions when their assistance is required.

> (*e*) After the forward representative has selected the site for the guns and sent or signalled back to them, he will make arrangements to enable them to come into action as soon after their arrival as possible. He will select targets, take ranges, and make any necessary calculations. He will therefore be accompanied by his range-taker.

4. When, after a period of movement, the situation again threatens to become stationary, every officer should make a detailed reconnaissance of the area round his guns, with a view to laying the foundation of a sound scheme of defence. Too often guns are found in places which were originally intended as halting places only, or in places to which they were forced in the exigencies of an action, to the neglect of better sites in the vicinity. If sub-section and section officers after local reconnaissance send in sketches, showing alternative positions and their fields of fire, on tracing paper of the same scale as the map in use, the Commanding Officers of Companies and the Divisional Machine Gun Commander will have at all times the raw materials of a good defensive scheme.

For Cavalry, *see* " Cavalry Training," Secs. 231-3.

40.—ATTACKS ON WOODS, VILLAGES, AND OTHER DEFENDED LOCALITIES.

1. The situation under consideration in this Section is that of any army retiring on a wide front and using the woods and villages which lie on its path as rear-guard positions, from which to arrest temporarily the progress of the pursuing forces. The object of the pursuer will be to expel the enemy from its defended localities with as little delay as possible, and drive his rear guards back on his main force, before that force has had time to settle down in a prepared system or to organize new defences of an elaborate nature

2. (*a*) Whenever these defended localities are sufficiently adjacent to each other they will undoubtedly be organised for mutual support by the long range fire of Artillery and Machine Guns.

(*b*) An operation against such a line will accordingly take the form, either of a simultaneous attack against the line on a wide front, or of attacks on certain localities to attract the enemy's attention, hold him to the ground, and wear down his power of resistance in combination with attacks on other localities, the capture of which will make it possible to envelop the enemy on either flank and cut off the retreat of his garrisons. (F.S.R., Sec. 103.)

The latter form of operation will, at the same time, probably allow a portion of the force which has broken through to push on rapidly and disorganize the retirement of the enemy's main body.

3. (*a*) As a rule, therefore, envelopment will be the preferable method; and the enveloping movements of the Infantry will be covered by the fire of Machine Guns from the front and flanks of the locality which is being surrounded. For this purpose a large number of the available guns will be employed with advantage for long range covering and searching fire, either direct or indirect.

(*b*) As the enveloping movements of the Infantry progress, Machine Guns will be moved to suitable positions on the flanks of the locality, from which enfilade and oblique fire can be brought against the flanks and rear of the defences.

(*c*) Long range fire from Machine Guns can also be used to cover the exits from the locality, thus preventing reinforcements and barring the lines of retreat to the defenders.

Fire of this kind will lower the morale of the defenders by producing that feeling of insecurity which always arises from a knowledge that the lines of retirement are under fire.

(*d*) In the case of villages, doors, windows, roofs, backs of houses, streets—especially those running at right angles to the attack—should be subject to the searching fire of Machine Guns.

(*e*) When the attacking troops have made good the edge, or some portion of the locality, some of the Forward Machine Guns may be brought up for their closer support. At the same time the fire power of these guns must not be wasted by placing them in positions where they are liable to be masked by our own troops, or in which Lewis Guns, owing to their portability, can do equal, if not better, work. The general rule will be that Lewis Guns are used in the more advanced positions, and the Machine Guns kept in the positions further back, where they can be best used to give supporting fire.

41.—DEFENCE OF WOODS, VILLAGES, AND OTHER DEFENDED LOCALITIES.

1. *Woods.*—(*a*) Isolated clumps are always to be avoided, as they invite concentrated artillery fire, but clusters of woods and woods of medium size, even though they are not part of a highly organized forest system, offer natural advantages for hiding Machine Guns. It is a long time before the trees are reduced to leafless sticks which afford no cover from view. Furthermore, trees stumps and undergrowth are ideal objects in which to fasten and hide wire.

(*b*) As, however, woods will always be subjected to more or less heavy shelling, the minimum of men should be retained to garrison them. This entails the plan being drawn up chiefly with a view to defence by Machine and Lewis Guns, covered by forward posts of Riflemen and Bombers. Through the smallness of their numbers the defenders will have plenty of elbow room, and thus be able to shift their positions and avoid those parts of the wood which are subjected to the heaviest shelling.

(*c*) In basing the scheme of defence on the fire of Machine and Lewis Guns, it must not be forgotten that while these weapons can deal with any attack which is above ground and visible, they are vulnerable to attacks by small parties, who, advancing unseen by covered approaches, penetrate into the position, and snipe or bomb the gunners at close range. In the daytime the defence can safely be left to the Machine and Lewis Guns, protected by a few posts of Riflemen and Bombers, but at night time, when it is most necessary to guard against surprise, adequate protection must be provided by Infantry Battalions.

2. *Villages.*—(a) The crowding of Machine Guns in villages that have not been carefully organized for defence by the construction of deep dug-outs, fortified cellars, and the like, only results in heavy loss of guns and personnel without compensating advantage.

(b) Positions will be sought, both in and out of the locality, from which all approaches to the village can be covered with belts of cross-fire.

(c) As envelopment is the most probable form of attack, Machine Guns will be posted to avoid this. Guns placed behind houses or hillocks in the outskirts of a village will often be found useful for this purpose.

(d) The use of houses or enclosures immediately in front of the village, which will give the enemy a commanding view of the village defences, must be denied to him.

(e) When Machine Guns are placed inside the village, great use can be made of a strong building as a protection against Artillery, the Machine Gun being sited behind the building and fired to a flank.

42.—OCCUPATION OF VARIOUS POSITIONS.

1. Machine Guns may be hidden in almost any position, but it is unwise to choose places which are either obvious or easy to recognize, such as cross roads or isolated objects. Guns should merge into the surroundings, and straight edges or distinct shadows should be avoided. When a position has been camouflaged, the success of the work will be best determined by reports from our own airmen.

2. Banks of rivers, canals, railways, ditches, folds in the ground, hedges, palings and walls may be used either as gun positions or as a covered avenue of approach.

3. Machine Guns in crops are difficult to detect from the same level, but unless the camouflage can be made to resemble the crops, the position will be easily picked out by enemy aircraft. A field covered with manure heaps or mounds of roots makes a better background.

4. If a barricade has been constructed across a road, Machine Guns should not be put on the barricade itself, but in a concealed position to a flank from which they can fire down the road or across and along the barricade.

5. Hay stacks and trees are more suitable for observation posts than for emplacements; but, in the same way as buildings in villages, they can be used to defilade Machine Guns which are located behind them and fire to either flank.

43.—ADVANCED GUARDS.

1. The duties of an advanced guard make it necessary that great fire power should be available when required. A large proportion of Machine Guns should therefore be allotted to advanced guards.

2. These Machine Guns should be well forward in the column, so that they may be able to get quickly into action; but if employed in support of the leading troops, they should be protected against surprise.

3. The principal duties of Machine Guns with the advanced guard are:—

       (i.) To assist in driving back enemy forces by rapid production of great fire power at the required point.

       (ii.) To assist in holding any position gained until the arrival of the main body.

       (iii.) To cover the deployment of the main body by holding the enemy on a wide front.

4. Machine Guns will normally be employed with the main guard, but with large forces it will often be of advantage to employ some Machine Guns with the vanguard. For example, with an advanced guard consisting of an Infantry Brigade, which has as much as a Battalion of Infantry acting with the vanguard, a normal distribution will be one section of Machine Guns with the vanguard, three sections with the main guard.

5. The section acting with the vanguard will be the Forward Guns mentioned in Sec. 38 para. 2 (*a*), and in the case of an attack being developed by the advanced guard, their *rôle* will be similar to that of the Forward Guns as described in Sec. 4. The three sections with the main guard

will be those mentioned in Sec. 38 para. 2 (*b*); and in case of an attack being developed by the advanced guard, their *rôle* will be similar to that of the Rear Guns as described in Sec. 5.

Whether their fire is direct or indirect, or whether a portion of them use direct fire and a portion indirect, will depend on the tactical circumstances of the particular situation, the nature of the ground, and the amount of Artillery at the disposal of the enemy.

44.—REAR GUARDS.

1. As a rear guard will usually be required to hold positions with the minimum of men, a large proportion of Machine Guns should be allotted to it.

2. Experience of war has shewn that well placed Machine Guns, supported by a few Infantry only, will frequently hold up an advance for long periods.

3. The method usually adopted by the enemy is to leave behind numerous Machine Guns, escorted by small parties of Infantry. These detachments occupy lines of defended localities in which, according to their orders, they hold out to the last, or up to a certain hour on a particular day.

4. In occupying a rear guard position with Machine Guns the same principles apply as for the defence in warfare of highly organised defences, the only difference being that, if the defences are of an improvised nature, the concealment of the guns will be of paramount importance.

5. The organization of the guns falls, as before, into two categories:—

(*a*) The Forward Guns, whose duties are generally those described in Sec. 21.

(*b*) The Rear Guns. These guns, using either direct or indirect fire, according to the circumstances, will be used to search with long range fire good approaches for hostile troops, and also to cover the withdrawal of the Forward Guns when this is necessary.

6. If it is required to fall back by stages, a portion of the Rear Guns, after having covered the withdrawal of the Forward Guns, can themselves become Forward Guns, the

Forward Guns taking up the work of the Rear Guns at some point further in rear.

In this way a continuous resistance will be offered to the hostile advance.

7. In addition to the ordinary principles of defence, the following points will be specially observed : —

(*a*) Covered lines of withdrawal will be reconnoitred.

(*b*) Limbered wagons will be close up to facilitate withdrawal, when the time for this comes. Pack transport will be found useful for the withdrawal of Forward Guns.

(*c*) Positions in rear will be chosen before the Machine Guns retire from their forward positions.

(*d*) A proportion of the Machine Guns will occupy the positions in rear, to cover the withdrawal of the Forward Guns. (*See* **paras. 5 and 6.**) Thus the withdrawal of the last gun can be covered.

8. A study of the foregoing considerations, in addition to the principles laid down in F.S.R., will enable Infantry Commanders to appreciate the nature of the resistance which they may expect to meet from enemy Machine Guns fighting a rearguard action in the open, and also will enable Machine Gun Commanders to deal skilfully with a situation in which a local retirement is temporarily imposed in the course of a general advance.

9. The principles outlined in Secs. 40-43 apply also to the employment of Machine Guns by Cavalry Units. *See* also Chapter VII.)

CHAPTER VII.

45.—THE TACTICAL HANDLING OF MACHINE GUN SQUADRONS.

1. The principles for the employment of Cavalry Machine Guns laid down in " Cavalry Training," Sections 225-236, hold good (with the exception of Sec. 225, Sec. 227, paras. 1 and 2; Sec. 228, para. 2, line 1; and Sec. 230, para. 4). The following Section is to be read as supplementary to, not substituted for, those Sections.

2. The general principles laid down in the foregoing chapters of this publication hold good where Cavalry are employed on foot.

3. *Co-operation.*—(i.) In order to ensure co-operation, the Machine Gun Commander must keep in the closest touch possible with the Commander of the Troops with whom he is acting. Thus, the Machine Gun Squadron Leader should ride with the Brigade Commander, and the section and sub-section leaders will keep in close touch with the Commanders of units to which they may be attached.

It is the duty of the Commander to allot a task to his Machine Gun Commander, who must be left to carry it out.

(ii.) Machine Guns must also co-operate with one another. To ensure this, the Machine Gun Squadron Commander will, both before and during an action, keep his sub-section officers fully informed of each other's orders and movements, and subordinate Machine Gun Commanders will neglect no opportunity of getting into touch with one another during the course of an action. Similarly, all Machine Gun Commanders will be responsible for gaining touch, and fighting in co-operation, with Machine Guns of other units acting on their flanks.

4. *Protection and Communication.*—The rule that the Commander of every body of troops is responsible for his own protection applies to Machine Gun Commanders. Since, however, for lack of personnel, a Machine Gun Commander is unable to detail reconnoitring and protective detachments and orderlies from the men under his command, his responsibility is limited to the duty of making a request to the Cavalry Commander under whose orders he is for such men to be attached to him as the situation demands.

5. *The Approach March.*—Owing to the necessity for careful reconnaissance and concealment and to the characteristics of the gun itself, Machine Guns take longer to come into action than Cavalry. Accordingly, the normal position of the Machine Gun unit during the approach march will be nearer the head of the column. Cavalry formations will be adhered to as far as possible, with a view to concealing the presence of Machine Guns.

6. *Distribution of Machine Guns.*—In actual fighting, a Machine Gun Squadron will rarely be employed as a unit. Machine Guns will be distributed among the units of the Brigade, the allotment of guns being governed by the following principles:—

(i.) Machine Guns will be attached to a unit only for a definite purpose.

(ii.) Generally, as many guns as possible will be kept in reserve, under the immediate control of the Brigade Commander. Once Machine Guns have been detached it is difficult to withdraw them should they be more urgently required elsewhere. Moreover, if Machine Guns are kept in hand until a definite occasion for their employment arises, the pack animals are spared much unnecessary fatigue.

(iii.) Sub-sections should not be broken up. Machine Guns are used with best effect in pairs, and a sub-section is organized with a view to its employment as a unit.

7. *Machine Guns in Action.*—(i.) In cases where ridden horses cannot approach reasonably near to gun positions, it will generally be found possible to have the gun and the first ammunition packs led up by dismounted gun numbers or pack leaders. A single horse can usually be placed under cover from view or fire, or both. This has the advantages of:—

(*a*) Sparing gun numbers unnecessary fatigue.
(*b*) Forming a mobile ammunition dump instead of a stationary one.

(ii.) When time allows and tools are available, guns will be dug in. Cover from view, however, often gives better protection than a hastily dug emplacement which may attract the enemy's attention.

(iii.) When guns are in position the Machine Gun Commander will allot targets and give general fire orders, but will not attempt to control directly the fire of one or more guns. Each detachment leader will control the fire of his own gun, while the Machine Gun Commander will remain free to watch the general situation, to make and receive reports, to maintain touch with his superior Commander and with the troops with whom he is co-operating, and to appreciate and conform to any change in the tactical situation.

APPENDIX I.

ORDERS FOR GUN POSITION No..........

1. Fire is only to be opened by order of the Gun Commander unless a sudden emergency arises, in which case the sentry will use his own initiative.

2. When relieving another gun team or sentry, the following facts will always be ascertained :—
   - (a) Whether the gun has been fired during the relief.
   - (b) If fired, what the target was.
   - (c) If fired, the emplacement from which it was fired.
   - (d) Whether any instructions have been received as to friendly patrols or wiring parties.

3. The sentry will always inspect the gun when taking over the position.

4. The sentry on duty must have an accurate knowledge of the targets shown on the fighting map.

5. In case of alarm, or a gas attack, the sentry will wake the gun team.

6. The gun will be cleaned daily, and the *points before firing* gone through both morning and night. The gun must be kept free from dirt, and in the trenches may be kept wrapped up in a waterproof sheet or bag. Such a covering must not prevent the gun being mounted for action immediately.

7. Ammunition, spare parts, and anti-gas apparatus will be inspected daily.
   The Gun Commander will be responsible that all anti-gas apparatus is always in position and in order.

8. The lock spring will never be left compressed.
   With the Vickers gun it is generally sufficient to half-load and then press the thumb-piece when mounting the gun at night. In order to open fire, it is only necessary to complete the loading motion and press the thumb-piece.

9. All dug-outs, emplacements and ammunition recesses belonging to the gun position must be kept clean and in good repair.

SPECIAL ORDERS FOR THIS GUN POSITION.

1. The S.O.S. signal is_____

2. Action on S.O.S._____

3. Action if enemy penetrates our front line_____

4.

5.

6.

LIST OF STORES BELONGING TO THIS GUN POSITION

Article	Number	Remarks
Fighting Map ...		
Barrage Chart ...		
Intelligence Summary		
Mountings (pivot, box, wooden base, etc.) ...		
Mills Grenades ...		
Picks ...		
Shovels ...		
Refuse tin ...		
Sundries ...		

Date ....

Machine Gun Officer.

APPENDIX II.

TYPES OF MACHINE GUN EMPLACEMENTS.

(a)

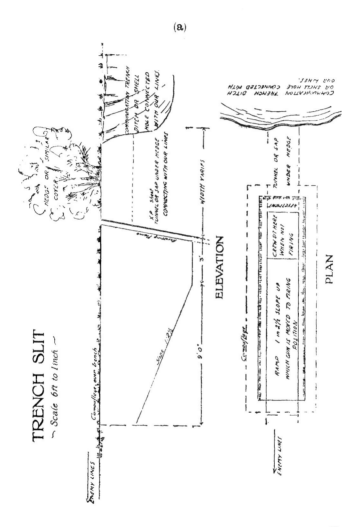

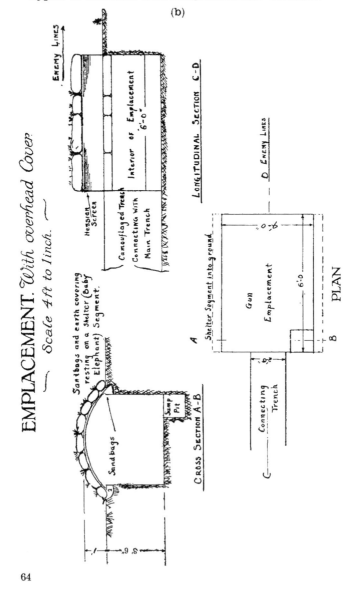

EMPLACEMENT. *With overhead Cover.*

Scale 4ft to 1 inch.

CROSS SECTION A-B

LONGITUDINAL SECTION C-D

PLAN

64

MACHINE. GUN EMPLACEMENT for BARRAGE WORK

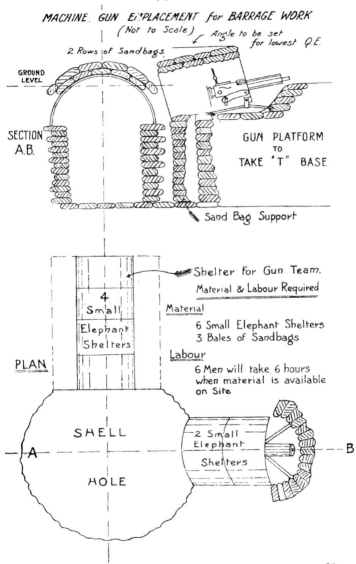

(Not to Scale)

Angle to be set for lowest Q.E.

2 Rows of Sandbags

GROUND LEVEL

SECTION A.B.

GUN PLATFORM TO TAKE "T" BASE

Sand Bag Support

Shelter for Gun Team.

Material & Labour Required

Material

6 Small Elephant Shelters
3 Bales of Sandbags

Labour

6 Men will take 6 hours when material is available on Site

PLAN

4 Small Elephant Shelters

A

SHELL HOLE

2 Small Elephant Shelters

B

APPENDIX III.

A.—OFFENSIVE OPERATIONS.

Typical Communications of Rear Guns on a Brigade Front.

Forward Guns communicate through the Infantry Battalions in whose area they are operating.)

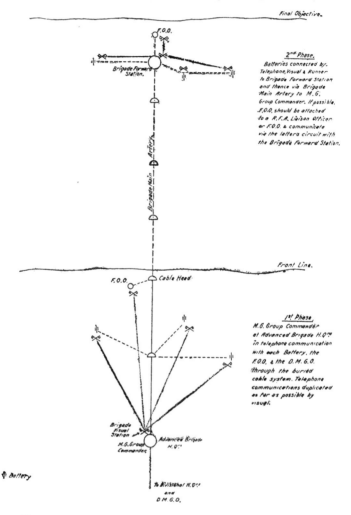

Appendix III.—*continued.*

B.—TRENCH WARFARE.

Typical Communications of Machine Guns on a Division Front.
(Forward sections communicate through the Infantry Battalions in whose area they are operating.)

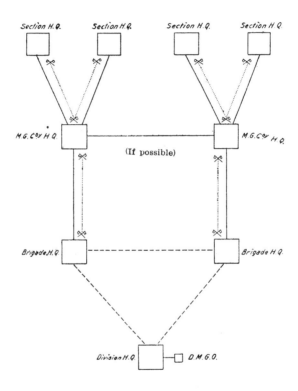

M.G. Lines _____
Infantry Lines _____
Visual (if possible) ✕✕✕✕✕✕

S.S. 192.]

[O.B. 1432A.

40/W.O./5678.

FOR OFFICIAL USE ONLY.

This Document is the property of H.B.M. Government, and the information in it is not to be communicated, either directly or indirectly, to the Press or any person not holding an official position in His Majesty's Service.

Not to be taken into Front Line Trenches.

THE EMPLOYMENT OF MACHINE GUNS.

PART II.

ORGANIZATION AND DIRECTION OF FIRE.

(ISSUED BY THE GENERAL STAFF.)

This publication cancels the instructions relating to Machine Guns in :—

C.D.S. 86 (June, 1915).
S.S. 106 (March, 1916).
S.S. 122 (September, 1916).
40/W.O./4032 (May, 1917).

January, 1918.

S.S. 192.]

[O.B. 1482A.
40/W.O./5678.

THE EMPLOYMENT OF MACHINE GUNS.

PART II.

ORGANIZATION AND DIRECTION OF FIRE.

(ISSUED BY THE GENERAL STAFF.)

January, 1918.

(B 18889) [3·18] Wt. w. 1845—PP 1644 10M 5/18 H & S P 18/187

THE EMPLOYMENT OF MACHINE GUNS.

PART II.

ORGANIZATION AND DIRECTION OF FIRE,

CHAPTER I.

CHAPTER II.

Map Work.

CHAPTER III.

Fire Direction.

NOTE.—The paragraphs marked in the text with an asterisk may be omitted on a first reading.

APPENDICES.

PART I. deals with "The Tactical Employment of Machine Guns."

INDEX.

A.

B.

C.

D.

E.

F.

G.

H.

I.

M.

N.

O.

V.

W.

Z.

NOTE.—The terms "Machine Gun," "Barrage," and "Battery" are used throughout this publication in the following senses :—

Machine Gun, to denote the ·303 Vickers Machine Gun.

Barrage fire by Machine Guns is the fire of a large number of guns acting under a centralized control directed on to definite lines or areas in which the frontage engaged by a gun approximates 40 yards. (*See* Sec. 17, para. 1.)

Battery:—A battery of machine guns only exists as a tactical unit in the motor machine gun branch of the Machine Gun Corps. In the Cavalry and Infantry branches the word is merely used as being the most convenient term for denoting a suitable number of guns placed under an officer as a fire unit for a particular purpose. (*See* Part I., Sec. 5.)

PART II.—ORGANIZATION AND DIRECTION OF FIRE.

CHAPTER I.

1.—MACHINE GUNNERS' MATHEMATICS.

A knowledge of the following simple mathematical facts is of great assistance in modern machine gunnery.

1. *Triangles.*

(i.) The three angles of a triangle are together equal to two right angles. Thus, if any two angles are known, the remaining angle can be found.

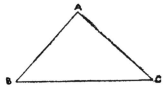

$$ABC + BCA + CAB = 2 \text{ right}$$
$$\text{angles} = 180°$$

(ii.) The exterior angle of a triangle is equal to the two interior and opposite angles.

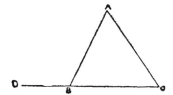

$$DBA = BAC + BCA$$

(iii.) If a line is drawn parallel to one side of a triangle, it divides the other side into proportional parts.

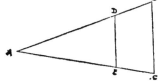

DE is parallel to BC

Then $\dfrac{AE}{AC} = \dfrac{AD}{AB} = \dfrac{DE}{BC}$

(iv.) *When the apex angle of a triangle is small,* the following is true for all practical purposes :—" If the base of a triangle be divided into a number of equal divisions and these divisions be joined to the apex, then the apex angle will be divided into the same number of equal angles."

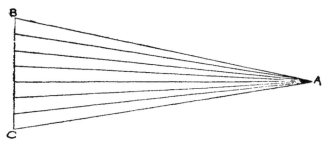

Example:—If BC be divided into seven equal divisions, the angle BAC is also divided into seven equal angles.

2. *Angles and parallel straight lines.*

(i.) When two straight lines intersect, the vertically opposite angles are equal.

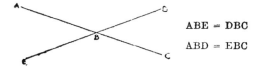

ABE = DBC

ABD = EBC

(ii.) When two parallel straight lines are cut by another straight line, the following are true :—

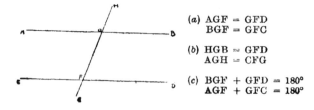

(a) AGF = GFD
   BGF = GFC

(b) HGB = GFD
   AGH = CFG

(c) BGF + GFD = 180°
   AGF + GFC = 180°

(iii.) If straight lines are parallel, they will still be parallel if all are switched through the same angle.

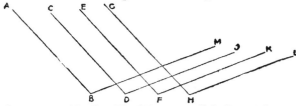

If the lines AB, CD, EF, GH are parallel, then if the angles B, D, F, H are equal, the lines BM, DJ, FK and HL will be parallel.

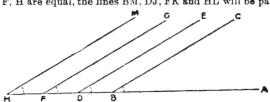

If the angles B, D, F, H are equal, then the lines BC, DE, FG, HM, are parallel.

*3. *The "V.I. over H.E." Formula.*

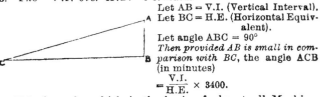

Let AB = V.I. (Vertical Interval).
Let BC = H.E. (Horizontal Equivalent).
Let angle ABC = 90°
Then provided AB is small in comparison with BC, the angle ACB (in minutes)

$$= \frac{V.I.}{H.E.} \times 3400.$$

This formula, which is the basis of almost all Machine Gun problems, is derived as follows:—

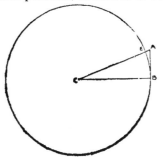

If the circumference of any circle be divided by the diameter, the same result is always obtained ; the circumference being 3·14159 times the diameter.

This figure 3·14159 is always denoted by π.

∴ Circumference = π × diameter.

$$= \pi \times 2R$$

where R is the radius.

7

Also the curved line BE is said to "subtend" the angle ECB at the centre. It is clear that a quarter of the circumference will subtend 90 deg. at the centre.

∴. The whole circumference will subtend $4 \times 90 = 360°$ at the centre.

Again, when AB is small compared with CB, the difference between AB and EB is negligible, and they can be taken as equal.

Now $2 \pi R$ Units subtend 360×60 minutes at the centre.

∴.   1 Unit subtends $\dfrac{360 \times 60}{2 \pi R}$,,   ,,   ,,

∴. AB (*i.e.* BE) units subtend $\dfrac{360 \times 60 \times AB}{2 \pi R}$ minutes at the centre ; which is the angle ACB.

∴. Angle $ACB = \dfrac{AB}{R} \times \dfrac{360 \times 60}{2 \times \pi} = \dfrac{AB}{R} \times \dfrac{360 \times 60}{2 \times 3 \cdot 14159} = \dfrac{AB}{R} \times 3438.$

As BED is any circle and ABC any triangle, this formula will be true for any triangle.

Thus—

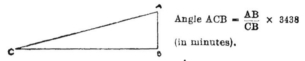

Angle $ACB = \dfrac{AB}{CB} \times 3438$

(in minutes).

Now AB represents the V.I., and CB the H.E.

∴. Angle in minutes $= \dfrac{V.I.}{H.E.} \times 3438.$

It will be more convenient in practice to use 3400 instead of 3438 and thus we get :—

Angle in minutes $= \dfrac{V.I.}{H.E.} \times 3400.$

The error introduced is 38 in 3438; *i.e.*, 1 per cent. approximately.

From the above formula, the following are easily obtained : —

$V.I. = \dfrac{Angle \times H.E.}{3400}$

$H.E. = \dfrac{V.I. \times 3400}{Angle}$

CHAPTER II.

2.—MAPS.

1.—TRUE NORTH, MAGNETIC NORTH, AND GRID NORTH.

On the older maps it was usual to divide the map by grid lines into squares, and to shew in the margin the True North and the magnetic variation from True North. It was therefore necessary, in using the map and compass for field work, to allow for three things:—

(a) *True North and Magnetic North are not the same.*

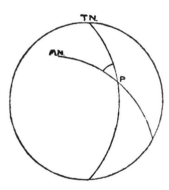

In this diagram T.N. represents the position of True North (at the North Pole), and M.N. represents the position of Magnetic North (a point at present in the northern extremity of North America).

If any point P is taken on the Globe, True North will be in the direction of T.N. and Magnetic North will be in the direction of M.N.

The angle TPM is the magnetic variation for the point P, and not only does this angle vary for different points, but it also varies year by year for any particular point.

(b) *Each country bases all its maps on one particular Meridian, and all other North and South lines are drawn parallel to this Meridian.* All other maps, such as the Trench Maps in use, are enlargements of portions of an original map thus compiled, *e.g.*, France bases its maps on the True North and South Meridian through Brussels, and the grid line through Brussels is True North and South.

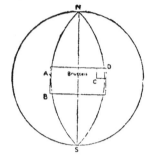

But if any other point **A** is taken, the line AB, though parallel to NS, is not True North and South. The curved line SAN is True North and South.

When a small part of this map is enlarged (*e.g.* CD) there is on grid line on the map which is True North and South. The deviation of the grid line from True North must therefore be allowed for, and it was usual to insert this on the maps at points E or F.

(*c*) *The magnetic variation of a particular compass is rarely the same as the correct variation* (as was shewn, *e.g.*, on the map) *for the locality in which it is being used.* The compass has an error which must be deducted from or added to the correct magnetic variation.

So long as reference is made to a True North, the above three things complicate work with map and compass, *e.g.*, suppose the machine gunner desired to lay out a line of fire by compass to a target shewn on the map. In obtaining the bearing from the map he had to allow first for the fact that the grid lines were not True North and South (and this was often difficult because the difference was not clearly shewn); and secondly for the error of his particular compass. Finally he had to remember whether the magnetic variation had to be added or subtracted. It is therefore better, as is now done on maps, to omit True North altogether, and work simply by Compass North and Grid North as follows:—

  (i.) Find the magnetic variation of your compass from the grid lines on map.

  (ii.) Measure all bearings with reference to the grid lines on the map.

(iii.) To convert a grid bearing into a compass bearing, add (in France) the magnetic variation of your compass: and conversely to convert a compass bearing into a grid bearing, subtract (in France) this variation.

To find the magnetic variation of a compass from the grid lines on the map.

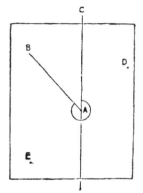

Select two distant points A and B, which are mutually visible on the ground and which are accurately marked on the map.

With the compass, take three separate bearings from A to B.

Take the mean of these three bearings as being the correct magnetic bearing of the compass from A to B (Say 324° 40′).

On the map, measure the bearing of AB with reference to the Grid North and South line passing through A (*i.e.*, AC). (Say 312° 20′).

Then the magnetic variation of that particular compass from this map, is 324° 40′ − 312° 20′ = 12° 20′.

Repeat the above process on a second object D, and again on a third object E. Three values for the compass variation will thus be obtained, and the average value may be taken as correct.

NOTE.—It will generally be found that the variations of the compass obtained from different points do not differ by more than 30 min., and the average value may be taken ; but where the variations differ by more than 1 deg. it will be necessary to note the variation in each direction. This difference is due to the compass cards being incorrectly centred. Where the error is considerable it is best to procure a new compass.

The above results can be conveniently arranged as follows :—

	Map Location from which bearings are taken	Map Location on which bearings are taken	Magnetic bearing	Mean Magnetic bearing	Grid bearing	Variation	Average Compass Variation
1.	R.21.d. 42·60	R.28.c. 10·14	(i.) 143° 10' (ii.) 143° 30' (iii.) 143° 20'	143° 20'	131° 40'	11° 40'	
2.							, say, 12° 5'
3.							

The compass variation must be found for every new map and in every fresh locality.

2. RESECTION.

The position on the ground being known, to find it on the map.

Accuracy is essential at every stage.

(i.) Find out your exact compass variation.

(ii.) Take several accurate bearings and take the mean as correct.

(iii.) Avoid metal likely to affect the compass readings.

(iv.) Draw carefully with a hard sharp pencil.

(v.) Whenever possible fix the position on the map by the detail close at hand rather than by resection.

Method A. Using compass.

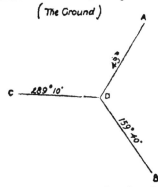

(The Ground)

The observer at D, wishing to fix the position of D on the map, selects two points A and B, visible on the ground and accurately marked on the map, and whenever possible a third point C, which checks the position of D, as fixed by AD and BD.

In order to obtain accurate results, the angles ADB, ADC, should not be greater than 130° nor less than 50°, and the points A, B, C. must be as close to D as possible.

The observer at D takes three compass bearings on A and finds the average bearing. He repeats this on B and then on C.

From these bearings he obtains the grid bearings to A, B and C, by subtracting his compass variations from each.

Object taken	Average Compass Bearing	Grid Bearing	
A.	45°	30° 40′	
B.	159° 40′	147° 20′	When the grid variation of the compass is 12° 20′.
C.	289° 10′	276° 50′	

To plot these resections, plot the bearings taken from D at the points identified on the map, with the protractor turned to the right for bearings over 180 deg. and turned to the left for bearings under 180 deg. This is quite simple with a protractor graduated in both directions.

13

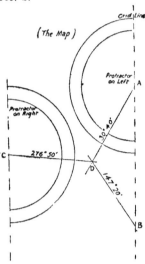

If the three straight lines drawn from A, B and C do not intersect at a point, it indicates (assuming the map to be correct) either that the grid variation of the compass has been inaccurately obtained, or that the drawing is inaccurate. If the triangle is large, the whole operation must be repeated; but if it is not much larger than a pencil point, the centre of the triangle may be taken as the position of D on the map.

Method B. Using a range-finding instrument.

This method is very useful when it is impossible to use a compass. The instrument must be accurately adjusted.

From D, the point whose position on the map is desired, take the range to three points A, B and C. These should be as near as is consistent with the minimum reading of the instrument (250 yards on the Barr and Stroud).

Then with a pair of compasses stretch the distance AD by the scale on the map, and with compass point at A, draw an arc. Repeat this for B and C, and the point of intersection of the three arcs will be the position of D.

In this case also, a triangle at D and not a point, indicates inaccuracy, and the same rule applies as in Method A.

Method C. Method of super-position.

Using a machine gun with direction dial, or a compass.

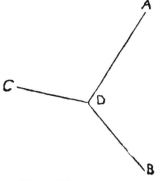

From D find the angles ADB, BDC and CDA by laying on A, B, C, in succession and reading off the angles on the direction dial.

Then on a piece of transparent paper draw a line AD, and from D draw a line DB so that the angle ADB = the angle ADB found above. Similarly draw DC making the angle CDB = the angle CDB found above.

Place this transparent paper on the map, so that DA passes through A on the map, DB through B on the map, and DC through C on the map. With a pin, prick through the point D, and the point thus obtained will be the position of D on the map.

NOTE.—The best results will be obtained when the points A, B, C are near D.

Instead of the Direction Dial the compass may be used. Take bearings on A, B and C. By subtracting the bearing of A from that of B obtain the angle ADB, and by subtracting the bearing of B from that of C obtain the angle BDC.

The position on the map being known, to find it on the ground.

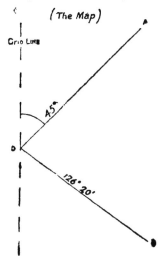

Select two points A and B which are recognisable on the ground and are marked on the map.

On the map join A and B, to D.

Through D draw a line parallel to the grid lines of the map, and by laying the centre of the protractor on D find the grid bearings from D to A, and B. Convert these bearings to compass bearings, by adding the compass variation.

Then with a compass variation of 12° 20′

From D the compass bearing to A = 45° + 12° 20′ = 57° 20′

From D the compass bearing to B = 126° 20′ + 12° 20′ = 138° 40′.

Proceed next on the ground to a point X, which you imagine is

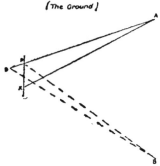

(The Ground)

near the point D, and take a bearing on A. Then facing A, if the bearing XA is less than 57° 20' you must move to your left; if the bearing XA is greater than 57° 20' you must move to your right. Suppose then, that the bearing XA is too small, you will move to the left until a point P is obtained such that the bearing PA is 57° 20'. Then the point D must be somewhere along the line PA. Place a stick at P, to fix the line PA. Take a bearing from P to B. If this is too great, then face B and move to the right along the line AP until a point D is obtained such that the bearing DB is 138° 40'.

Then D is the point required, because the bearing DA is 57 deg. 20 min., and the bearing DB is 138 deg. 40 min., which was required.

NOTE.—(i.) As a final check, the bearing on a third point should be obtained.

(ii.) Whenever possible, fix the position D by detail close at hand.

When the obliteration of all landmarks makes resection impossible, it is sometimes possible to get the position fixed by the help of the Field Artillery or a Field Survey Company.

3.—SCALES.

The word scale is used to denote the proportion which a distance between any two points on a map bears to the horizontal distance between the same two points on the ground. This same proportion can be expressed as a fraction which is called the Representative Fraction (R.F.).

Thus R.F. $= \dfrac{1}{20,000}$ indicates that 1 unit on the map represents 20,000 of the same unit on the ground.

A sketch should always have a scale attached, which, for convenience of use, should be about 6 in. in length.

To construct a scale of 12 inches to the mile, showing divisions of 100 yards and sub-divisions of 20 yards:—

First, find how many yards are represented by 6 inches.

12 inches represents 1,760 yards.

∴ 6 inches represents 880 yards.

Then, as the scale must be divided into hundreds of yards, make the scale to represent 800 yards.

Secondly, find what length of line will represent 800 yards.

1,760 yards are represented by 12 inches.

∴ 1 yard is represented by $\dfrac{12}{1,760}$ inches.

∴ 800 yards are represented by $\dfrac{12}{1,760} \times \dfrac{800}{1}$ inches.

Then the scale must be $\dfrac{12 \times 800}{1,760} = 5\cdot45$ inches.

Thirdly, draw a line 5·45 inches, and divide it into 8 equal parts, each division representing 100 yards. Divide the left division into 5 equal parts, each representing 20 yards.

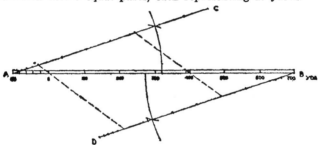

Method of dividing the scale into parts:—

Draw AB = 5·45 inches.

Draw AC = 4 inches (this length being easily divisible by 8), and divide AC into eight equal parts.

Draw BD = AC and parallel to AC and divide it also into eight equal parts.

Then by joining the corresponding divisions of AC and BD, the line AB will be divided proportionately as desired.

Similarly, by dividing the left divisions of AC and DB into 5 equal parts and joining up the corresponding sub-divisions, the left division of AB will be subdivided as desired.

17

4.—CONTOURS.

1. DEFINITION.

" The representation of an imaginary line running along the surface of the ground, at the same height above mean sea-level throughout its length."

Only a certain number of these lines are drawn on the map, and the heights of intermediate points must be estimated. Generally on our maps of 1/10,000 and 1/20,000, contours shew each vertical distance of 10 metres, which is called the Vertical Interval between the contours.

2. EXAMINATION OF A MAP.

(i.) Contours indicate the relative steepness of slopes.

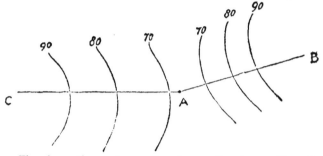

The closer the contours, the steeper the slope. Thus the slope along BA will be steeper than that along CA.

(ii.) Contours indicate the form of the surface of the ground.

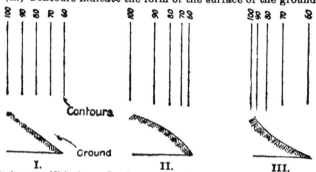

I.	II.	III.
Contours equidistant. Slope uniform.	Contours becoming closer, going from high to low ground Surface is convex and there will be dead ground.	Contours becoming wider, going from high to low ground. Surface concave, and there will not be dead ground.

(iii.) From contours the gradient, or steepness of slope, can be calculated.

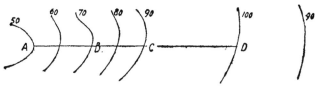

(AB = 500 yards).

Example:—The slope A to B is required.

Suppose AB = 500 yards. (= ZY).

B is 20 metres = 22 yards above A. (= XY).

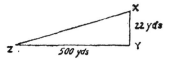

Then the gradient is "22 in 500," or written as a fraction $= \frac{22}{500} = \frac{1}{22 \cdot 7}$ The steepness of the slope can also be measured by the angle XZY. (*See* Section 45.)

Angle XZY (in minutes) $= \frac{XY}{ZY} \times 3,400 = \frac{22}{500} \times 3,400 = 149!$

Practical uses.

(*a*) Knowing the gradient, it is possible to judge whether a road on a reverse slope in the enemy's territory will be used by transport or not; for it is very improbable that a gradient greater than 1-10 (*i.e.*, 6 deg.) will be used. From this we can decide whether to fire on the road or not.

(*b*) The steepness of a slope will decide in the selection of routes for transport.

If the gradient is 1-20 (*i.e.*, 3 deg.), even on a good road, time must be allowed to breathe the horses.

On a gradient of 1-10 (*i.e.*, 6 deg.), a horse can only draw one quarter of the load it can draw on the level.

(*c*) Knowing the slope of the ground fired on, several deductions can be made of probable fire effect. (*See* "Fire effect in relation to slope of ground." Sec. 49, para. 2.)

(iv.) From contours, one can find whether two points are mutually visible.

Example:—See Diagram in (iii.).

Is the point D visible from the point A? C is the point likely to cause the obstruction.

Now AC = 950 yards, and AD = 1,600 yards.

C is 40metres = 44 yards above A, and D is 50 metres = 55 yards above A.

∴ the angle of sight from A to C = $\frac{44}{950} \times \frac{3,400}{1}$ = 157 minutes;

and the angle of sight A to D = $\frac{55}{1,600} \times 3,400$ = 117 minutes.

Then as the angle of sight from A to C is greater than that from A to D, the point D is not visible from A.

The practical use of the above would be in selecting routes of advance either for troops or for transport. For instance in the previous diagram, suppose we hold C and the enemy holds A, it would be safe for troops to cross D, although D is the highest point in the vicinity, because D cannot be seen from A.

(v.) From a contoured map, sections of the country can be made.

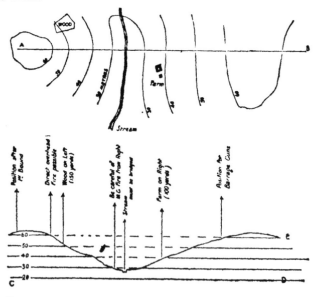

In the above contours, to make a section from A to B:—

Join AB on the map.

Draw CD = AB, marking the points where each contour cuts AB.

Draw DE to some convenient scale to shew the vertical intervals of the contours. Plot in the vertical section of the ground: and then insert details that are likely to be of practical value.

A section thus constructed will be useful, for example, for shewing troops the kind of ground over which they have to advance, especially if aeroplane photographs are difficult to obtain.

For purposes of study, the construction of such sections is one of the best ways of appreciating the different problems connected with contours.

CHAPTER III.

FIRE DIRECTION.

5.—THEORY OF FIRE.

1. TECHNICAL TERMS.

Axis of the bore.—An imaginary line following the centre of the bore from breech to muzzle.

Line of sight.—The straight line passing through the sights and the point aimed at.

Trajectory.—The curved path taken by the bullet in its flight to the target.

Cone of fire.—The figure formed in the air by the trajectories of the outermost shots of a burst of fire.

Culminating point.—The highest point of the trajectory above the line of sight.

Its position is approximately 6-10 of the range.

First catch.—The point where the lowest bullet has descended sufficiently to strike the head of a man, whether mounted, standing, kneeling, lying, etc.

First graze.—The point where the lowest bullet, if not interfered with, will first strike the ground.

Beaten zone.—The area of ground beaten by a cone of fire.

(i.) The length is great compared with the width.

(ii.) The dimensions of the beaten zones of the Vickers gun have never been satisfactorily measured, and recent experiments with average guns and average firers indicate that the beaten zones are longer and narrower than the official dimensions in Appendix IV., Table I.

Effective beaten zone.—The area of ground beaten by the best 75 per cent. of the shots.

Drift.—The term used to express the lateral deviation of the bullet, brought about by its gyroscopic action, after it has left the barrel. Experience indicates that for purposes of machine gun fire drift need not be taken into consideration.

Angle of sight.—The angle contained between the line of sight and the horizontal plane

Angle AGB = angle of sight for target A.
Angle BGC = ,, ,, ,, ,, ,, C.

By convention, the angle is said to be positive (+) when the target is above the H.P., and is negative (−) when the target is below the H.P., through the gun position.

Angle of tangent elevation.—The angle between the axis of the bore and the line of sight.

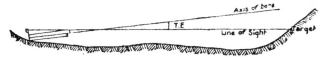

T.E. is the angle of tangent elevation.

Angle of quadrant elevation.—The angle between the axis of the bore and the horizontal plane.

Relation between angles of quadrant elevation (Q.E.), angle of tangent elevation (T.E.), and angle of sight.

   (a) Target above gun.

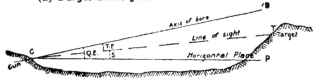

By definition:—
Angle BGP = Angle of quadrant elevation.
Angle BGT = Angle of tangent elevation.
Angle TGP = Angle of sight.
Then QE = TE + S.

i.e., When the target is above the gun, the angle of quadrant elevation is equal to the angle of tangent elevation, plus the angle of sight.

23

(b) *Target below gun.*

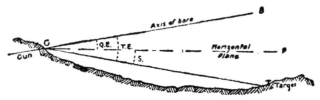

By definition :—

Angle BGP = Angle of quadrant elevation.
Angle BGT = Angle of tangent elevation.
Angle PGT = Angle of sight.
Then QE = TE − S.

i.e., When the target is below the gun, the angle of quadrant elevation is equal to the angle of tangent elevation minus the angle of sight.

Generally, then, the relation can be expressed by the following formula :—QE = TE $\overset{+}{-}$ S.

Angle of descent.—The angle which the tangent to the trajectory, at the point of impact, makes with the line of sight.

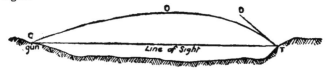

GT = line of sight. | DT is the tangent to the
GOT = trajectory. | trajectory at the point of
T = point of impact. | impact.
                  Then angle DTG = Angle of descent.

*   For all practical purposes this can be calculated in the following manner :—

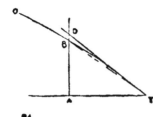

OBT is the trajectory.

AT = line of sight.

DT = tangent at point of impact.

Then if AT = 100 yards, the trajectory BT will be practically coincident with the tangent DT, and we can assume that the angle BTA = DTA.

The distance BA can be found for any range, from the Trajectory Table 2 A. (Appendix IV.)

Then angle BTA $= \dfrac{BA}{AT} \times 3,400 =$ Angle of Descent.

Example:—Find the angle of descent for 1,800 yards.

From Table 2 A find the height BA, *i.e.*, the height of the 1,800 yards trajectory at 1,700 yards. This equals 12 yards.

Then angle of descent $= \dfrac{BA}{AT} \times 3,400 \; \dfrac{12}{100} \times 3,400 = 408$ min.

(Compare Table I., Column 3).

Dangerous space.—For one bullet, the dangerous space is the distance between the first catch and the first graze. In a burst of machine gun fire the *danger zone* is an area equal to the beaten zone, *plus* the area formed by the dangerous space for each bullet.

2. FIRE EFFECT IN RELATION TO SLOPE OF GROUND.

On level ground the length of the beaten zone varies considerably with the range; but also at any particular range the length of the beaten zone varies with the inclination of the ground to the line of sight.

The reverse slope.

Suppose AB is the length of the beaten zone along the line of sight GAB. Then it is clear that if the reverse slope AC be engaged, the beaten zone produced along this reverse slope by the same cone of fire will be AC, and will exceed AB.

Suppose, also, that DA represents the length of the dangerous space when firing along GAB, then EA will represent the length of the dangerous space when firing on the reverse slope.

Along the line of sight, therefore, fire effect will be produced for a distance DB, but on a reverse slope fire effect will be produced for a distance EC, and this distance (as will be shown later) will greatly exceed DB.

Sec. 5.

On a reverse slope the ratio of the length of AC to that of AB at any range can be found as follows :—

$$\frac{AC}{AB} = \frac{\text{Angle of descent}}{\text{Angle of descent} - \text{Angle of slope of ground}} = \frac{FBA}{FBA - BAC}$$

Example :—Range 2,000 yards. Slope of ground 1 in 14.

NOTE.—If the ground slopes 1 in 14, the angle of slope $= \frac{1}{14} \times 3,400 = 251'$.

Also angle of descent at 2,000 yards = 541',

$$\frac{AC}{AB} = \frac{541}{541 - 251} = \frac{541}{290} = 1\cdot8.$$

Therefore AC is 1·8 times (*i.e.*, nearly twice) the length of AB at 2,000 yards when the ground slopes 1 in 14.

The forward slope.

Again let AB represent the length of the beaten zone along the line of sight GAB. Then AC will represent the length of the beaten zone produced by the same cone of fire along the forward slope AC.

Also, if DA represents the dangerous space along the line of sight, EA will represent it along the forward slope.

In all cases on a forward slope, the length of ground effectively engaged (*i.e.*, EC) will be less than on the line of sight (*i.e.*, DB).

On a forward slope, the ratio of the length of AC to that of AB is found as follows :—

$$\frac{AC}{AB} = \frac{\text{Angle of descent}}{\text{Angle of descent} + \text{Angle of slope of ground}} = \frac{CBA}{CBA + CAB}$$

Example :—Range 1,500. Slope of ground 1 in 12 (*i.e.*, angle of slope = 298').

$$\frac{AC}{AB} = \frac{251}{251 + 298} = \frac{251}{549} = \frac{5}{11}$$

Thus AC will be less than half the length of AB, at 1,500 yards when the ground slopes 1 in 12.

3. CLIMATIC INFLUENCES AND THEIR ALLOWANCES.

The following are the normal atmospheric conditions for the Sighting of Small Arms : —

> (i.) Barometric pressure. 30 inches. (Sea level.)
> (ii.) Temperature. 60 deg. Fahrenheit.
> (iii.) Still air.
> (iv.) A horizontal line of sight.

(A) Atmospheric variations that affect elevation.

When the barometer rises above 30 inches, more elevation than is normally required for the distance will be necessary, owing to the greater resistance offered to the bullet by the denser atmosphere. If the barometer falls below 30 inches, as is the case in damp weather, or at a height above sea level, less elevation will be required, as the atmosphere will offer reduced resistance to the bullet. In the same manner the bullet meets with less resistance in hot weather when the thermometer is high, and greater resistance in cold weather when it is low.

(i.) The following rule for correction in case of variation in barometric pressure is approximately correct:—

> *For every inch the barometer rises or falls above or below 30 inches, add or deduct 1½ yards for each 100 yards of range.*

When the barometer rises, add—*vice versâ.*

Example:—Range, 2,000 yards. Barometer, 29 inches.

Allowance = 1 × 1½ × 20 = 30 yards. (Deduct this.)
Corrected range = 1,970 yards.

(ii.) The following rule for correction in case of variation ir temperature is also approximately correct : —

> *For every degree which the temperature rises or falls above or below 60 deg., deduct or add 1-10 yards for each 100 yards of range.*

Example :—2,100 yards. Temperature, 50 deg.

Allowance $= \frac{1}{10} \times (60 - 50) \times (\frac{2,100}{100})$

$= \frac{1}{10} \times \frac{10}{1} \times \frac{21}{1} = 21$ yards. (Add this.)

Corrected range = 2,121 yards.

(iii.) The following rule for correction in case of head or rear winds is approximately correct : —

$$\frac{\text{Allowance}}{\text{in yards}} = \frac{\text{Speed of wind in miles per hour} \times \text{Time of flight.}}{2}$$

If an oblique wind, divide the speed by two, and call it head or rear, as the case may be. (*See* also Note (iv.) below.)

Example:—Wind from left front at 20 M.P.H. Range 1,950 yards. This wind is equivalent to a head wind of 10 M.P.H.

Then allowance $= \dfrac{10 \times 6}{2} = 30$ yards.

Corrected quadrant elevation = 1,980 yards.

Table 4, Appendix IV., has been introduced to save these lengthy calculations, and, with practice, the corrected range for any atmospheric conditions can be worked out in less than half a minute.

(*B*) *Atmospheric variations that affect direction.*

A side wind acts on the greater surface of the bullet, and has consequently more influence on its flight than a wind blowing from the front or rear.

One must also note that, owing to the increased time during which the bullet is exposed to the effect of wind, and to the height attained in its flight, the allowance for wind at long range is out of all proportion to that necessary at short range.

The following table will act as a rough guide:—

RANGE.	LATERAL ALLOWANCES. (*cf.* Table 5, App. IV.)					
	Mild. 10 M.P.H.		Fresh. 20 M.P.H.		Strong. 30 M.P.H.	
Yards.	Yards.	Minutes.	Yards.	Minutes.	Yards.	Minutes.
500	1	5	1½	10	2	15
1,000	3	10	6	20	9	30
1,500	6	15	12	30	18	45
2,000	12	20	24	40	36	60
2,500	24	30	48	60	72	90

NOTES:—

(i.) Halve the allowances for oblique winds. (*See* Note iv.)

ʃ(ii.) For direct fire the minutes of angle should be used in conjunction with a card and string, in order to obtain an

auxiliary aiming mark. If there is no aiming mark available use the following rough rule :—

> Assume the following factors :—Mild 2. Fresh 3. Strong 4. Then multiply the range by the appropriate factor, and the first figure of the answer gives the taps required.

Example :—Fresh wind at 1,500 yards :
   1,500 × 3 = 4,500 : Order 4 taps.

(iii.) For indirect fire make the allowance in minutes of angle, either by the Deflection Bar Foresight, or with a " T " Aiming Mark placed 9½ yards away, so that one inch lateral distance will represent 10 minutes.

(iv.) The rule that oblique winds should be halved in order to find the equivalent head, rear, or side wind is only very approximately correct, and when greater accuracy is required the following table should be employed to determine what ratio of the wind will act in the direction of the line of fire, *i.e.,* affect the elevation, and what ratio will act at right angles to the line of fire, *i.e.,* affect the direction.

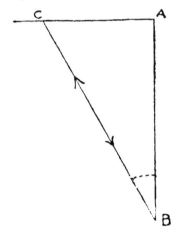

BA gives the line of fire.

The direction of the wind may be CB or BC.

Angle A.B.C.	Ratio of wind affecting elevation.	Ratio of wind affecting direction.
10°⎫ 20°⎭	1	$\frac{1}{4}$
30°⎫ 40°⎭	$\frac{3}{4}$	$\frac{1}{2}$
50°⎫ 60°⎭	$\frac{1}{2}$	$\frac{3}{4}$
70°⎫ 80°⎭	$\frac{1}{4}$	1

Example:—An oblique head wind of 20 miles per hour is blowing at an angle of 30 deg. to the line of fire. Then this is equivalent to a head wind of 20 x $\frac{3}{4}$, *i.e.*, 15 M.P.H., and a side wind of 20 x $\frac{1}{2}$, *i.e.*, 10 M.P.H.

(C) Effect of not having a horizontal line of sight.

As previously stated, one of the normal conditions under which a machine gun is sighted is that the line of sight shall be horizontal. When this condition obtains, the forces acting on the bullet cause it to travel on its greatest curve, and the elevation for any given distance must therefore be given to the gun.

When firing up or down hill, the tangent elevation required gets less as the angle of sight increases, until when firing vertically upwards or downwards no tangent elevation is required at all.

It is very improbable that it will be found necessary to engage a target at an angle of sight of more than 10 deg. (except hostile aircraft, which is provided for on the special sights issued), and it also happens that no allowance need be made for angles of sight less than 10 deg. Hence no table for correction is necessary.

4. RESULTS OF RECENT EXPERIMENTS.

Experiments made to examine the behaviour of the bullet at ranges of about 3,000 yards proved that fire at over that range will be of very little value.

The shape and size of each beaten zone would appear to vary with each burst fired, and the area beaten is always very large. This is no doubt due to the fact that the bullets attain

a great height, and are influenced by many varying air currents.

The bullet also appears to fall sideways, sometimes pointing to the right and sometimes to the left, indicating that it has ceased to rotate with its point foremost.

The power of penetration was also tested, and the bullet was able to penetrate into 1½ inches of soft wood.

On the other hand, barrage demonstrations at 2,500 and 2,600 yards prove that accurate and effective firing can be produced at these ranges.

Other experiments showed that new barrels shoot higher than old ones, and that after 20,000 rounds the bullets drop short about 5 per cent. of the range.

6.—COMBINED SIGHTS, SEARCHING AND TRAVERSING.

1. PERMISSIBLE AND PROBABLE ERRORS IN RANGE FINDING.

(*a*) *Permissible error in range finding.*

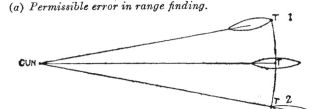

Suppose a target is being engaged which is 1,000 yards away. Then if the centre of the effective beaten zone hits the target (T) the lowest shot of the E.B.Z. will hit the ground 70 yards short of the target, and the highest shot 70 yards beyond the target, because the length of the E.B.Z. is 140 yards.

If now the centre of the E.B.Z. falls 70 yards short, the highest shot only will hit the target (T1).

Or if the centre of the E.B.Z. falls 70 yards beyond the target (T2), only the lowest shots will hit the target.

It is clear then, that if an error of more than 70 yards is made in obtaining the distance to the target (T), the whole of the fire effect will be lost, because the target will not be hit. Seventy yards can be called the permissible error, and it is half the length of the effective beaten zone.

In general, the length of beaten zone decreases, as the range increases, and consequently the permissible error *decreases* as the range increases.

(b) *Probable error in range finding.*

Whether the fire be direct or indirect, the range to any given target can rarely be obtained with complete accuracy, and the magnitude of this probable error depends on the method employed in obtaining the range.

The following table will act as a rough guide:—

(i.) Using range-finding instrument, 5 per cent. error.

(ii.) Using a range card built up from key ranges, the key ranges being found by instrument, and the intermediate ranges by judging distance   ...   . 10 per cent. error.

(iii.) Judging distance (by eye) ... 15 per cent. error.

(iv.) Using 1/10,000 map ...   · ·⎫ Within 5 per cent.
(v.) Using 1/20,000 map ...   ...⎭

This means that we can never look upon our target as a point, for there will always be a certain length in which the target may lie.

For Example:—Suppose with a range-finding instrument we decide that the range to a certain target is 1,000 yards.

Then as an error of 5 per cent. may have been made either way, the target may be anywhere between the points A and B; and to ensure hitting the target, we must produce fire effect on the whole of the line AB.

AB in this case is twice the probable error, and = 2 × 5 per cent. of the range.

It is clear that the greater the range, the greater the probable error will be. For example, in this case considered above, the probable error is 50 yards, but if the range had been 2,000 yards, the probable error would have been 100 yards.

To consider the permissible and probable errors together : —

Example:—Range 2,000 yards, using range-finding instrument.

Ground to be searched = 2 × 5% of range = 200 yards.
Permissible error = 35 yards.

Example:—Range 1,500 yards, using key ranges.

Ground to be searched = 2 × 10% of range = 300 yards.
Permissible error = 40 yards.

Example:—Range 1,000 yards, using judging distance method.

Ground to be searched = 2 × 15% of range = 300 yards.
Permissible error = 70 yards.

Therefore, in practically all cases, it is necessary to increase the depth of the beaten zone considerably in order to ensure fire effect.

There are two methods of doing this:—

(*a*) Combined sights.
(*b*) Searching.

2. COMBINED SIGHTS.

Definition:—The method of engaging any required depth of ground by applying simultaneously overlapping zones of fire from two or more guns.

The depth of the beaten zone is increased by ordering different elevations to be used by each gun, while each uses the same aiming mark.

In direct fire these different elevations are put on by ordering each gun to fire with a different elevation on the tangent sight. In indirect fire the same effect is produced by ordering a different quadrant elevation for each gun.

Rule for combined sights.

" Always use as many guns as possible, with 100 yards' differences if the error in range finding is probably considerable, and with 50 yards differences if the error in range finding is probably small."

Explanation of the result produced.

Example:—Range 1,500 yards (as found by range-finding instrument) 3 guns available.

50 yards differences will be used. (Rule above).

Then for direct fire, the order will be:—
"1450 yards – 50 yards differences."

For indirect fire, the order will be:—
"Elevation 2° 5' – 10' differences.

(The angle of sight is assumed to be nil: the tangent elevation for 1,450 yards = 2° 5', and that for 1,550 yards = 2° 25'.)

In each case the result at the target will be as follows:—

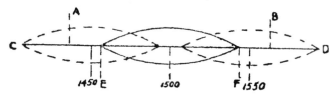

AB = 150 yards = Ground to be searched = (2 × 5% of range).
CD = Depth of E.B.Z. produced = 180 yards.
EF = Length of each E.B.Z. = 80 yards.

From this diagram it is clear that the likelihood of hitting the target (which lies between A and B) is greatly increased, but, as the fire is spread out, the density will be greatly diminished. Consequently, whenever observation of fire can be obtained, the controller must cease using combined sights, and fire with all the guns at the correct elevation to hit the target.

"Combined sights" is specially useful when surprise effect is desired, because each portion of the ground in which the target probably lies is beaten simultaneously.

NOTE.—When the target is itself a depth of ground, *e.g.*, a wood, combined sights will be maintained, even though fire effect on a particular part of the target has been observed. (*See* para. 4 below.)

3. SEARCHING.

Definition:—The method of engaging any required depth of ground by applying successively overlapping zones of fire from one gun.

On comparing this method with combined sights, it will be seen that searching is of little value when surprise effect is desired, because, whereas in combined sights each part of the target is engaged simultaneously, in searching each part of the target is engaged successively.

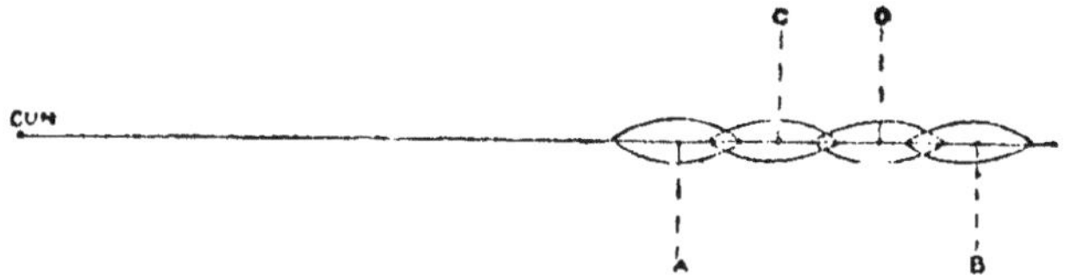

Suppose the target lies somewhere between the points A and B; then to ensure hitting it, the whole distance AB must be engaged.

The firer places a burst on A, then elevates his gun and places another on C, then on D, and continues until the whole line has been covered.

It requires much skill on the part of the firer to avoid gaps between bursts, and proficiency can only be obtained by constant practice on the 25 yards' range.

The firer is taught on the 25 yards' range to turn the elevating wheel after firing a burst, so that the next burst of fire is two inches above the first. This is called the " Normal " or " Two-inch " turn.

G is the gun position.

A and B the positions on the target of two bursts of fire, the necessary elevation being given to the gun after the first burst to raise the point of impact to B, which is two inches above A.

Using the V.I. formula:—

$$\text{The angle B.G.A.} = \frac{2 \times 3400}{25 \times 36} = 8 \text{ minutes (nearly)}$$

i.e., the two-inch turn elevates the gun eight minutes.

Alterations in elevation are made by turning the elevating wheel, and it must be impressed on the firer that the required turn is a very small one.

For example, when firing at 1,100 yards (tangent elevation 73 min.), an elevation of 13 min. will throw the beaten zone 100 yards forward (because the tangent elevation for 1,200 yards is 86 min.). As two normal turns of the wheel elevate the gun by 16 min., the firer, if not properly trained, will probably elevate for more than this between bursts, and so leave gaps between the beaten zones on the target.

The firer should also be trained to apply his fire in suitable volume. Suppose the target is 1,200 yards away and a burst of 5 rounds is fired. The length of the ground covered by that beaten zone may be 240 yards, and the width is 7 yards, and it is clear that the effect of 5 bullets on such a large area will be very small. Bursts of 20 or 30 rounds should be fired, or even more, if there is reason to suppose that the target is a dense one.

When searching is being employed to overcome errors in range-finding (the object at present under discussion) the following is the procedure:—

> The controller decides between what limits the target lies (say, between 1,200 yards and 1,500 yards).
> He then orders range to near limit (*i.e.*, 1,200 yards).
> Then he indicates the target.

No. 1 aims at target with smaller range (1,200 yards).
Controller then orders range to far limit (1,500 yards).

No. 1 alters his sights to 1,500 yards without elevating the gun.

No. 1 fires bursts and elevates until aiming at the target with 1,500 yards.

Then, providing that the target lay between 1,200 yards and 1,500 yards, it will have been effectively engaged.

4. There is also another important use of combined sights and searching, which arises when the target is itself longer than the beaten zone which can be produced by one gun.

In this case the total length of ground which must be searched can be found by adding the length of the target to twice the probable error.

When using combined sights, a point in the *centre* of the target will be employed as an aiming mark (if the centre is not visible, the near end), and the controller will decide from the number of guns available and from the length of the target, whether he should use 100 yards or 50 yards differences in order to cover the whole target.

If the target is on a forward slope it will generally be advisable to use 100 yards' differences, in order to counterbalance the shortening of the beaten zone which arises when firing on such a slope.

Example:—AB is a road, the near end being 1,200 yards and the far end 1,600 yards from the gun.

Then although a distance CD (400 yards) is covered *along the line of sight* (because all guns will have the same line of sight to T), only a part of the road AB will be covered, namely EF.

In order to cover as much of AB as possible, spread out the fire by ordering 100 yards' differences.

If such a target be engaged by the method of searching, the existing rule needs modification. This rule states:—"The firer will aim at the near end of the target with the range to hit it. Then run his tangent sight slide to the range to the far end. Then fire and elevate until aiming at the *near* end."

Such a process will only bring fire effect on the whole target when the far end of the target is on the prolongation of the line of sight to the near end.

Example:—AB is a long target on a forward slope, A being 1,400 yards, and B 1,800 yards from the gun. If the

37

existing rule be followed, the firer will elevate until aiming at A with 1,800 yards on his sights, but although his fire would, in the absence of ground at D, go to a point C, 1,800 yards along the line of sight, it will not touch B the far end of the target.

In such an instance the rule must be altered; the firer should fire and elevate until aiming at the *far* end of the target.

4. TRAVERSING.

Definition.—The method of engaging any required width of ground by distributing laterally against it the fire of one or more guns.

The normal way of engaging a wide target is to aim at one extremity, fire a burst and then tap and fire alternately until the whole target has been covered.

The firer is taught on the 25 yards' range the required strength of tap to cause the horizontal distance between bursts to be two inches on the target at 25 yards. This is called the " Regulation two-inch tap." It is equivalent to a traverse of eight minutes (*see* " Two-inch turn," page 35).

If the object in view is to bring fire effect on a belt or an area of ground (as in a barrage) this method is very effective. But if the target is a thin line of extended infantry, or a trench running at right angles to the line of fire, traversing is wasteful. In such cases the best fire effect is obtained by firing in enfilade, or as obliquely to the target as possible.

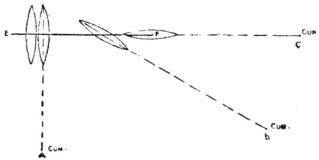

EF is a line of extended infantry at 1,000 yards.

The EBZ is 140 yards long and 1.7 yards wide.

Then if EF is engaged from A (*i.e.*, frontally), only the width of the EBZ can be counted as effective (1.7 yards).

If EF is engaged from C (*i.e.*, in enfilade), the whole
length of the EBZ (*i.e.*, 140 yards) can be counted as effective.
The fire effect produced will then be 80 times as effective from
C as from A.

From B (*i.e.*, obliquely), the fire effect will be greater
than from A, and the effect will increase the nearer the fire
approaches to enfilade.

It will also be seen that the time taken to cover the whole
Target EF from B will be much less from B than from A.

Every endeavour, therefore, should be made to reduce
traversing to a minimum, and to engage targets from oblique
or enfilade positions.

NOTE.—In the above example EF is looked upon as one
single target, which it is better to engage EF from C than
from any other position.

If, however, the object in view is to make a certain line
EF impassable to the enemy, it is better to engage it frontally,
provided sufficient guns are available to do this effectively,
because then the enemy
will be bound to pass
through a deep belt of
ground beaten by machine
gun fire, whereas if the
same object is attempted
by enfilade guns, only a
very narrow belt of
ground is effectively en-
gaged.

5. OBLIQUE TRAVERSING.

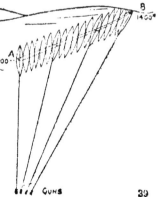

Consider a target such as
AB, running obliquely to the
line of fire. Such a target is
very often likely to demand
attention (a road, hedge, or
trench), and it is one of the
most difficult to engage.

39

The best way is to use a combination of combined sights, searching and traversing.

For example, with four guns, order:—
        1,100 yards, 100 yards' differences.
        Road—Four points of aim.
        Oblique traversing.
        Fire.

Each No. 1 will then traverse along his own portion of the target, keeping his line of sight on the target.

It will then be unnecessary to order any one gun to use different elevations.

6. SWINGING TRAVERSE.

This is a method of engaging a wide target by firing continuously, and at the same time distributing the fire along the whole target.

It necessitates loosening the traversing clamp, which allows the gun to vibrate more than in ordinary tap traversing, and it is therefore not so accurate as the normal method of traversing.

Consequently the swinging traverse should not be used except at dense targets which are not more than 500 yards distant.

7.—DIRECT OVERHEAD FIRE.

1. It has long been an accepted principle of infantry tactics that, whenever the ground permits, an advance should be assisted by fire directed at the enemy over the heads of the assaulting troops.

For this type of fire action, in which the safety of the troops whose advance is being covered is the primary consideration, the machine gun, by reason of its fixed mounting and the close grouping of its fire, is characteristically fitted.

The safety of the attacking troops is ensured by the employment of a " Safety Angle," the magnitude of which depends on the range to the target.

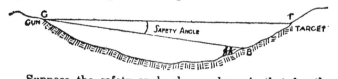

Suppose the safety angle shown above is that for the range GT. Then it is safe for the firer at G to fire on the target until the advancing troops meet the line GB.

2. RULES FOR DIRECT OVERHEAD FIRE.

(i.) If the range to the target is 1,000 yards or under, the safety angle is 30 min.

If the range to the target is between 1,000 and 1,500 yards, the safety angle is 60 min.

If the range to the target is over 1,500 yards, the safety angle is 100 min.

NOTE.—If the ground is comparatively flat between the gun and the target, closer support may generally be given by using the methods of indirect fire, if it is possible for these methods to be used.

(ii.) Direct overhead fire must not be employed if the attacking troops are more than 2,000 yards from the gun.

(iii.) The range to the target must be known to within 5 per cent.

(iv.) A worn barrel or a worn tripod must not be used.

(v.) No. 1 must be a good firer.

(vi.) The tripod must be well dug in.

(vii.) The target and our own troops must be clearly visible.

Notes on the preceding rules.

* (i.) The calculation of the safety angles given in Rule (i.) is based on the following allowances:—

(*a*) That a maximum error of 5 per cent. of the range may have been made in range-finding.

(*b*) That the lowest bullet may fall short an additional 10 per cent. of the range on account of bad holding, aiming, worn barrel or defective ammunition.

(*c*) Over and above the allowance for errors in range finding and firing, allowance is also made for the known distance of the lowest shot of the cone below the centre shot.

(ii.) In Rule (ii.), there is no limit to the range from gun to *Target.*

(iii.) Rules (iii.) to (vii.) are practical precautions for minimising the errors allowed for in Rule (i.), and thus making the safety of the attacking troops absolute.

(*) (iv.) In addition, the controller will allow for climatic conditions, especially for head winds.

3. METHODS OF APPLYING SAFETY ANGLES.

Method I.—By graticules.
Card.

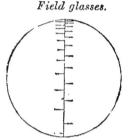

Field glasses.

(Card held at the distance denoted on the card from the eye.)

(View through graticuled glasses.)

It should be noticed at the outset that graticules were designed for indirect fire (*see* Sec. 9), and consequently the use of graticules for direct overhead fire is more or less accidental.

But it so happens that on looking through graticules (whether on a card or on graticuled glasses) the angle formed at the eye by the zero line and the 600 yards line is 28 min.

Similarly the angle between zero and 1,000 is 62 min., and the angle between zero and 1,300 yards is 101 min.

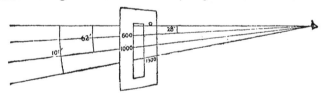

These three angles are very close approximations to the angles laid down in Rule 1, and the error involved in using them as 30 min., 60 min. and 100 min. is negligible.

The procedure is to align the graticule so that the line from the controller's eye through the zero mark is on the target.

Then the line passing through the 600 yards' graticule will give the safety limit when the range to the target is 1,000 yards or under (*i.e.*, safety angle of 28 min.).

The line passing through the 1,000 yards graticule will give the safety limit when the range to the target is between 1,000 and 1,500 yards (*i.e.*, safety angle of 62 min.).

The line passing through the 1,300 yards graticule will give the safety limit when the range to the target is more than 1,500 yards (*i.e.*, safety angle of 101 min.).

Method II.—Special safety angle graticule card.

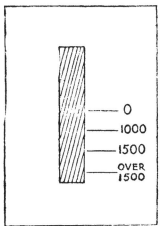

The card is aligned so that the line from the controller's eye through the zero mark is on the target.

Then the line marked "1,000" will give a safety angle of 30 min. The line marked "1,500" will give a safety angle of 60 min., and the line marked "over 1,500" will give a safety angle of 100 min.

(Card held at the distance denoted on the card from the eye.)

The controller, observing Rule 1, and knowing the range to the target, will know which line to use for any particular instance.

Method III.—Tangent sight method.

In the two methods given above, the controller alone knows how far it is safe to support the advance. If he should become a casualty, the firer will be in danger either of supporting the advance beyond the safety limit, or of ceasing fire too soon, in which case the attacking troops will lose the effect of his covering fire.

A second objection to the two previous methods is that only three safety angles are permissible. This in itself is unsound, because the safety angle necessarily varies with every variation in the range.

Both difficulties are overcome by the following method:—

> *Stage 1.*—The firer lays on the target with the range to hit it. Then, without moving the gun, he runs up his sights 300 yards higher, and finds at which point on the ground he is now aiming.
>
> This position on his new line of sight becomes his aiming mark, and he continues firing, constantly checking his aim on it, until his line of sight is touched by the advancing troops, when he ceases fire. The fire up to the present will have been directed on the target, because initially the gun was laid on the target with the range to hit it.
>
> *Stage 11.*—The firer now raises his sight another 200 yards and elevates the gun, aims at (*i.e.*, takes a line of sight on to) the target, and fires until the attacking troops reach the target which is their objective, when he ceases fire if our troops intend advancing further. By so doing, fire effect is produced on the ground beyond target, and this will help to neutralize the fire of the enemy's support.

At close ranges Stage II. is unsafe, unless the procedure is modified as follows:—

> At the completion of Stage I., when the attacking troops have touched the line of sight to the auxiliary aiming mark, No. 1 runs his tangent sight slide to 1,300 yards (unless already as high or higher), lays on the target and fires until the attacking troops reach the target.

Example:—Range to target, 800 yards.

Lay on the target with 800 yards on the sights.

Alter tangent sight to 1,100 yards (*i.e.*, 300 yards higher), use the point M thus found, as aiming mark.

Fire until the attacking troops touch the line G.M.

Then cease fire, *and set sights at 1,300 yards.*

Aim at the target, and continue firing until the advancing troops reach T. Then cease fire.

4. CONCLUSION.

In the absence of factors which obstruct the field of view (mist, smoke screens, the smoke and dust caused by artillery, etc.), the foregoing methods of direct overhead fire are technically reliable. But because one or other of these factors either is or may be present, arrangements for indirect fire should be made as stated in Part I., Section 15, and they should be of the following nature:—

> Once the gun has been laid on the target, an auxiliary aiming mark should be put out for the purpose of maintaining elevation and direction, and the maximum time during which the advance can be supported should be obtained either by estimating the rate of advance or by obtaining it from the artillery time-table. Thus, the point up to which the attacking troops can advance with safety being known, it can be decided how long fire may safely be directed on the target.

8.—INDIRECT FIRE (GENERAL).

1. *Indirect fire is fire directed by any other means than laying the gun over the sights on to the target.*

Indirect fire may be carried out by guns controlled:—

(*a*) Singly.

In this case the line of fire of each gun is laid out separately, and without reference to the line of fire of another gun.

(*b*) Batteries.*

In this case the lines of fire of the guns constituting the battery are laid out in parallel directions, and these form a basis from which the controlling officer can issue an order producing:—

(*a*) Distribution of fire along any line.

(*b*) Concentration of fire on any locality.

Where possible, registration should always be carried out.

As this is often impossible, reliance must be placed upon the theoretical rules which underlie the application of indirect fire.

Unless these rules, their limitations and applications are clearly understood, accurate indirect fire is impossible, the safety of the troops, over whose heads the fire is being directed,

---

* See Note at end of Index.

may become endangered, and the expenditure of S.A.A. is not justified.

For example, unless the officer carrying out the fire nas a knowledge of his probable errors in direction and elevation, he may either : —

(a) By searching an area unnecessarily large (in order to obtain fire effect on the target) obtain a very small material result; or

(b) By searching an area too small, miss the target altogether.

If the necessary care is taken, accurate indirect fire can be carried out with the present equipment of the gun.

In order to test this possibility, tests have been carried out over a period of six months. These have been undertaken by different squads of officers under instruction, under varying weather conditions.

The targets were six 10 ft. by 3 ft. screens placed one behind the other, but on the side of a hill, so that one shot could not hit more than one target. The map location of the targets was given to the officers carrying out the test.

In all cases elevation was placed on the gun by clinometer and one belt was fired.

No traversing was allowed, as the tests were designed to show the errors in direction.

The following results were obtained : —

Gun position fixed by detail on the map.

Range, 1,200 yards.

I.—Direction by compass.

No. of tests, 20. Average error in direction, 30 min.

II.—Direction by reference object.

No. of tests, 22. Average error in direction, 15 min.

Gun position fixed by resection.

No points nearer than 1,000 yards were allowed to resect from.

Range, 1,450 yards.

III.—Direction by compass.

No. of tests, 17. Average error in direction, 15 min.

IV.—Direction by reference object.

No. of tests, 21. Average error in direction, 30 min.

The results show that with care the degree of error should not exceed 30 min., therefore a total traverse of 1 deg. should include the target.

To carry out indirect fire with accuracy and rapidity entails a high standard of professional efficiency on the part of the officer. He must have a thorough knowledge of:—

(a) Maps.

(b) The compass and its " characteristics."

(c) The tables and graphs which give—

(i.) Angles of elevation and descent.

(ii.) Dimensions of cones and beaten zones.

(iii.) Methods of determining quadrant elevation.

(iv.) Methods of determining clearances.

(v.) Allowances for atmospheric conditions.

(d) Methods of laying and fire control.

(e) The technical equipment in use.

(f) Probable errors.

2. Indirect fire will be dealt with under the following headings:—

Indirect fire of guns controlled singly.

I. Without the map (i.e., where a 1/20,000 or larger scale contoured map is not available).

(a) By graticules.

(b) By angle of sight instrument or director.

II. With the map (i.e., where a 1/20,000 or large scale contoured map is available).

(a) To obtain direction.

(b) To obtain elevation.

Indirect fire of guns controlled in batteries.

I. With the map.

II. Without the map.

Maintaining laying.

Clearances.

Night firing.

Searching reverse slopes.

Errors.

Barrage fire.

9.—INDIRECT FIRE OF GUNS CONTROLLED SINGLY.

1. INDIRECT FIRE WITHOUT THE MAP.

A. *By use of graticules.* (*See* Sec. 7.)

The following instruments are required:—

    (i.) Barr and Stroud range-finder.

    (ii.) Field glasses in which graticules are cut across the focal plane, or graticule cards.

Procedure.

(i.) Move to a position from which the target can be observed. (This should not be more than 6 feet above the gun, and at approximately the same range from the target.)

(ii.) Obtain range to target.

(iii.) Select a suitable aiming mark, visible to the gun, which is vertically above or below the target, and in alignment of gun and target.

(iv.) Observe the target so that the graticule representing the range falls across the target.

(v.) Note which graticule cuts the aiming mark, and the corresponding range.

(vi.) Order the No. 1 of the gun to put this range on his tangent sight and lay on the aiming mark.

This method gives accuracy of direction but not great accuracy of elevation. The fire effect is greatly enhanced when observation can be obtained.

NOTE 1.—As the range on the sight is not the range to the target, the fire cannot be corrected by ordering " up 50 " or " down 50," etc. (since the ratchet is uniform, and an alteration of one click elevates or depresses the gun through the same angle, no matter what position of the slide, the correction is applied by alteration by clicks).

There are roughly as many clicks in the ratchet of the tangent sight as there are hundreds of yards in the range, at all ranges below 1,500 yards.

For example, if the range is 1,200 yards, and fire is 100 yards short, the controlling officer orders " up 12 clicks." The No. 1 moves his slide up 12 clicks and relays on the auxiliary aiming mark.

NOTE 2.—Where a suitable auxiliary aiming mark can be seen above or below the target, this method is useful to bring fire to bear on a target which is visible through glasses, and is difficult to indicate to the No. 1.

B. *By ·the TOG method.*

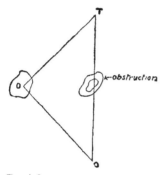

The figure shows the
Gun position, G.
Target position, T.
Observation station, O.
The following instruments are required :—

1. B a r r and S t r o u d range-finder.
2. Director and angle of sight instrument, or s o m e m e a n s o f measuring the angle TOG and angles of sight.

Procedure.

To obtain direction :—

After selecting the gun position the Controlling Officer goes to a position from which he can see both the gun and the target, and—

(1) Takes ranges to the gun and to the target with the Barr and Stroud.

(2) Measures the angle TOG.

This is done :—

(*a*) With a director, by laying it on G and T in turn, and noting the angle swung through.

(*b*) Without a director by taking bearings to G and to T, and then the difference between these bearings is the angle TOG.

The ranges OT, OG, and the angle TOG being known, it is now simple to find the range GT, and the angle TGO.

This is done:—

      (*a*) With the " plotter."

      (*b*) Without the " plotter." Draw a line to represent the range OT, set off the angle TOG with a protractor, and mark off the point G, so that OG represents the range OG. Measure the angle TGO with the protractor.

Order the gun to lay on the observation station and lay off the angle TGO. An aiming post is now set out, and the gun is laid for direction.

To obtain elevation :—

      Take the angle of sight from O to T = t°

                             O to G = g°

This is done with an " angle of sight " instrument.

      To find the angle of sight from G to T = S° use the formula :—

$$S° = \frac{t° \times OT - g° \times OG}{GT}$$

NOTE.—*See* Theory of Fire, Sec. 49, para. 1.

The angle of sight to a point is positive where that point is above the position of observation, negative where it is below.

Having found the angle of sight S, find the TE for the range GT and the Q.E. from the formula.

$$Q.E. = T.E. \pm S.$$

Order this Q.E. to be placed on the gun.

The gun is now laid for direction and elevation. Where observation can be obtained fire can be corrected by ordering " 30 min. left," etc. – " up 20 min."

The fire control is best carried out by telephonic communication from O to G—or where this is not possible, by visual signalling.

Where the observation post is in the direct line from the gun to the target, direction can be obtained by placing posts, and elevation as follows:—

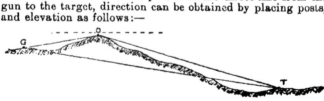

Let —

    OT = Range from crest to target.
    OG = Range from crest to gun.
    $t°$ = Angle of sight from crest to target.
    $g°$ = Angle of sight from crest to gun.

Then angle of sight from gun to target = $S°$

$$S° = \frac{t° \times OT - g° \times OG}{GT}$$

and GT = OG + OT approximately.

This " TOG " method can be easily adapted to guns employed in a battery. (*See* Sec. 10, para. 5.)

2. INDIRECT FIRE WITH THE MAP.

The map must be at least 1/20,000 and contoured.

A. *To obtain direction.*

Method 1. *By map and compass.*

(i.) *The position of the gun on the ground must be accurately fixed on the map.*

This is done either :—

    (*a*) From the detail on the ground and comparing this with the detail on the map ; or

    (*b*) if this is not possible, by resection.

Any of the methods described in Sec. 2, para. 2, may be used.

Where time permits greater accuracy is ensured by employing one method and checking with another.

It may be possible to obtain the aid of a Field Survey Company where a very accurate location is necessary.

The use of oblique aeroplane photographs has been found helpful when moving guns forward to positions already sited in territory previously hostile.

(ii.) *The magnetic bearing from the gun to the target must now be found.*

To do this :—

    (*a*) Draw a line on the map from the gun position to the target.

    (*b*) Using the protractor, measure the bearing this line makes with any North and South Grid line. This is the grid bearing from the gun to the target.

    (*c*) Add the magnetic variation of the compass from the North and South Grid lines. The result is the magnetic bearing from the gun to the target.

NOTE 1.—(*c*) Applies only to places where the magnetic variation is West.

If the variation is East, subtract instead of add.

NOTE 2.—The variation of the compass must be determined for each compass for the particular map in use, and should be constantly checked. (*See* Sec. 2, para. 2.)

(iii.) *To lay the gun on the magnetic bearing so obtained.* This can be done in the following ways:—

(*a*) Place a post (not more than 6 inches high) in the gun position and place the compass on the top of the post. Rotate the compass until the card reads the required bearing.

Align an aiming post on this bearing using the hair line on the compass. Place the gun with the centre of the cross at the bottom of the socket, immediately over the post, and lay on the aiming post.

(*b*) By use of the compass tower.

See Appendix VIII.

(*c*) It may often be impossible owing to the presence of iron to use a compass from the gun position itself. Take the compass out more or less in the required line of fire, either in front of, or behind the gun.

Two cases now occur:—

1. *Compass in front of gun.*

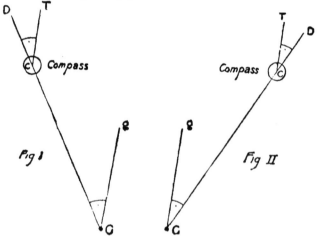

The figures show:—

1. CG the bearing from compass to gun.
2. CD the back bearing.
3. CT the bearing on which the gun is required to fire.
4. Gg the line of fire obtained by laying off the angle gGC, which = the angle TCD.

NOTE.—Since the angle gGC = the angle TCD gG is parallel to CT, and the gun is laid on the bearing required.

Rule.

1. Take the compass 30 to 50 yards in front of the gun more or less in the direction of fire. Lay the gun on the compass. Take the bearing CG on to the gun.

2. Obtain the back bearing CD.

3. Obtain the angle between this bearing and the one on which it is required to lay the gun (*i.e.*, CT). This is the angle TCD.

4. The observer at C now turns his back on the gun, and faces the direction CD—if the bearing on which it is required to fire the gun (*i.e.*, CT) lies to his right, the gun lays off the angle TCD to the right—and if to his left, the angle TCD is laid off to the left.

The gun is now laid on the required bearing in the direction Gg, which is parallel to CT; and an aiming post is put out.

Example:—To lay a gun on a magnetic bearing of 7 deg.

Supposing—

(i.) It is found that bearing CG = 170°.
(ii.) Adding 180° the back bearing CD = 350°
(iii.) The difference between a bearing of 350° and 7° = 17°.
(iv.) Facing CD the bearing CT lies to the right. Therefore the gun lays off 17° to the right,

Or again it may be ound that—

 (i.) Bearing CG = 210°.
 (ii.) Subtracting 180° the back bearing
   CD = 30°.
 (iii.) The angle TCD = 30° − 7° = 23°.
 (iv.) Facing CD the bearing CT lies to
   the left; therefore the gun lays
   off 23° to the left.

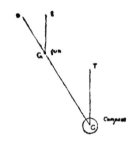

Compass behind gun.

The figures show:—

 (i.) CG the bearing from compass to gun.

 (ii.) CT the bearing on which the gun is required to fire.

 (iii.) Gg the line of fire obtained by laying off the angle gGD, which = the angle TCD.

NOTE.—Since the angle gGD = the angle TCD, gG is parallel to CT, and the gun is laid on the bearing required.

Rule.

1 Take the compass 30 to 50 yards behind the gun more or less in the prolongation of the line of fire, lay the gun back on to the compass from the *foresight* through the *backsight*.

Take the bearing CG on to the gun.

2. Obtain the angle between this bearing and the one on which it is required to lay the gun (*i.e.*, CT). This is the angle TCD.

3. The observer at C, now faces the gun. If the bearing

on which it is required to fire the gun lies to his right, the gun lays off the angle TCD to the right—and if to his left, the angle TCD is laid off to the left.

The gun is now laid on the required bearing in the direction Gg, which is parallel to CT; and an aiming post is put out.

Example:—To lay a gun on a magnetic bearing of 27 deg.

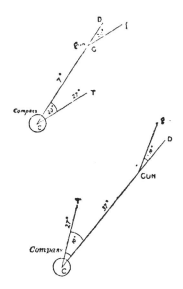

Supposing:—

1. It is found that bearing CG = 7 deg.

2. Difference between a bearing of 27 deg. (*i.e.*, CT) and 7 deg. = 20 deg.

3. Facing CD the bearing CT lies to the right, therefore the gun lays off 20 deg. to the right.

Or, again, it may be found that:—

1. Bearing CG = 37 deg.

2. Difference between a bearing of 27 deg. (*i.e.*, CT) and 37 deg. = 10 deg.

3. Facing CD the bearing CT lays to the left, therefore the gun lays off 10 deg. to the left.

Method 2. By map and reference object.

(i.) The position of gun on the ground must first be accurately fixed on the map. (*See* Sec. 2, para. 2.)

(ii.) A reference object, which is both marked on the map and visible from the gun, is next selected. A line is drawn on the map.

     (*a*) from the gun position to the target—G.T.; and

     (*b*) from the gun position to the R.O. —G.R.

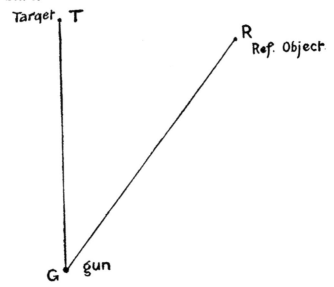

The angle TGR is now measured with a protractor. The gun lays on the R.O. and taps off the angle TGR, and an aiming post is put out in the direction obtained. The gun is now aligned on the target.

NOTE 1.—The angle TGR may be measured with a protractor without drawing any lines—but these are an aid to accuracy.

NOTE 2.—Where the position of the gun can be found from the detail on the ground, all errors arising from the use of the compass are avoided.

Method 3. By map, reference object, and compass.

A modification of Method 2 is necessary where no suitable reference object exists which is marked on the map and is visible from the gun.

Select a reference object on the ground, or, if necessary, place one out. Take the compass bearing from the gun position to the reference object.

Find from the map the bearing on which it is required to fire the gun. Find the difference between these bearings and lay off the angle obtained from the reference object.

NOTE.—*Effect of atmospheric conditions on direction.*

After the gun has been laid for direction by any of the methods given above, it is necessary to make the correction for wind. To find the allowance *see* Sec. 5, para. 3.

This allowance is put on the gun either by tapping off the required angle on the " T " shaped aiming post or by using the bar foresight.

B. *To obtain elevation.*

(i.) *On the map*, measure the range from the gun to the target and note:—

(*a*) The gun contour.

(*b*) The target contour.

The difference between the gun contour and the target contour is the vertical interval (V.I.).

(ii.) The quadrant elevation is now found by the formula:—

Q.E. = T.E. $\pm$ S. (*See* Sec. 5, para. 1.)

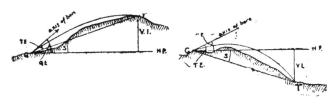

To obtain the angle of sight use the formula:—

Angle of sight in minutes $= S = \dfrac{V.I.}{H.E.} \times 3400,$

where V.I. = Vertical interval,
H.E. = Range,

and both are measured in the same unit.

In France, where the vertical intervals are in metres and the ranges in yards, the following may be used:—

$S \text{ (in minutes)} = \dfrac{V.I. \text{ (metres)}}{H.E. \text{ (yards)}} \times 3750.$

Example:—

Range = 1,700 yards and T.E. for 1,700 = 177′.

Gun contour = 20 yards.

Target contour = 50 yards.   Therefore V.I. = 30.

$$S = \frac{30}{1700} \times 3400 = 60'.$$

QE = TE + S
 = 177 + 60 = 237′,

or again if range = 1,700 yards,
 Gun contour   = 50 yards,
 Target contour = 20 yards,

$$S = \frac{30}{1700} \times 3400 = 60'$$

QE = TE − S
 = 177′ − 60′
 = 177′.

(iii.) In order to save calculating the angle of sight and combining it with the tangent elevation to find the quadrant elevation, Tables 3A and 3B (Appendix IV.) have been compiled.

(These tables are compiled from the formula:—

$$S = \frac{V.I.}{H.E.} \times 3438:$$

the factor 3438 being more accurate than 3400, which gives an error of 1.2 per cent.)

Graph No. 1, Appendix V., allows the quadrant elevation to be read off without calculation of the angle of sight.

(iv.) *Before placing elevation on the gun the correction for atmospheric influences must be first made and the correction added to or subtracted from the Q.E., according as the correction is positive or negative.*

To find the correction *see* Sec. 5, para. 3.

(v.) *To put the elevation on the gun.*

Elevation is put on the gun with the clinometer:—

 (*See* Appendix XI.: Adjustment of clinometers).

  1. Set the clinometer to the required reading.

  2. *Without holding,* place the clinometer on the tangent sight bed and elevate or depress the gun until the bubble is central. Move up the tangent sight slide until the point of aim is on the auxiliary aiming mark.

3. Take the holding and relay on the auxiliary aiming mark, using the elevating wheel, and *not* moving the tangent sight slide.

NOTE.—This method obviates the error arising from a difference in holding when putting on elevation and when firing.

10.—INDIRECT FIRE OF GUNS CONTROLLED IN BATTERIES.*

Laying and fire control where 1/20000 or larger scale contoured map is available.

(To be read in conjunction with Barrage Drill, Sec. 17, para. 7.)

1. All the guns of one battery are laid on parallel lines of fire initially, and zero aiming posts are placed in position. These lines are called the zero lines of fire of the battery, and form the basis from which the line of fire of each gun is taken. The methods of obtaining parallel lines of fire are explained in para. 4 of this Section, but where the nature of the ground admits, these lines should be checked by registration.

The guns are numbered from right to left, and the position of one gun is fixed as accurately as possible on the map. This gun is known as the directing gun, and is generally the left gun, to facilitate control   The choice of the zero line is arbitrary, but if the left gun is directing, it is generally the line from that gun to the left end of the first barrage line—or in the case of a S.O.S. barrage, to the left end of this S.O.S. line.

The zero line of the directing gun is laid out by any of the methods given in Sec. 9, para. 1, A, and elevation is obtained as described in Sec. 9, para. 2.

When a battery engages a target, the fire of each gun is laid at equal intervals along it.   Each gun traverses 1 deg. either side of its line of fire, except:—

(i.) When concentrated fire is ordered.

(ii.) Where the concentration of guns is great, *i.e.*, one gun to between 30 and 40 yards of front, when the total traverse is 1 deg.

(iii.) Where the concentration of guns is thin, and a traverse of 1 deg. either side is insufficient to ensure that no gaps are left.   In this case a traverse of twice the angle of distribution should be ordered.

---

* *See* note at end of Index.

This traverse prevents gaps by causing:—

> (i.) The fire of neighbouring guns to overlap.
> (ii.) The fire of neighbouring batteries to overlap.

At the same time, as the angle of traverse is small, different guns can have different quadrant elevations when the nature of the target demands it.

The fire is controlled by either—

> (*a*) Shutter.
> (*b*) Whistle.

The former has been found the more effective method.

2. DISTRIBUTION OF FIRE.

Where the frontage of the target as viewed from the battery, is greater than that of the battery, it is necessary to distribute the fire of the battery from their parallel lines, in order to lay the fire of each gun at equal intervals along the target.

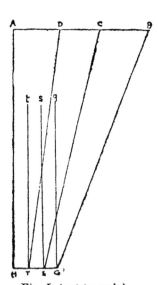

Fig. I. (not to scale).

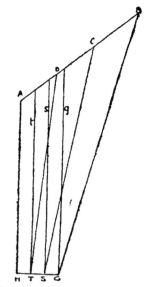

Fig. II. (not to scale).

These figures shew the lines of fire of a 4-gun battery:—

    (*a*) On their parallel zero lines.

    (*b*) After distribution of fire along:—

        (i.) A frontal target.

        (ii.) An oblique target.

The angle DT't is the *angle of distribution of the battery for the target AB.*

The angle CSs = twice the angle DTt.

The angle BGg = three times the angle DTt.

Example :—If angle DTt = 1°

        angle CSs = 2°

        angle BGg = 3°

Measurements of this angle are taken to the nearest 10 min.

If the zero line of the left gun (*i.e.*, directing gun), is not directed on the left end of the target, this gun is switched through an angle so as to direct its fire on to the left end of the target. This angle is called the " switch angle," and before distribution of fire along the target, all guns are ordered to lay off this angle from their zero lines. This angle is measured by a protractor, or read from the fighting map.

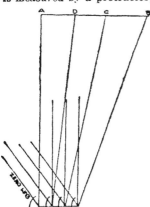

Angle of switch.
Fig. III. (not to scale).

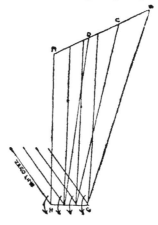

Angle of switch.
Fig. IV. (not to scale).

Sec. 10.

These figures shew the lines of fire of a 4-gun battery :—

   (a) On their parallel zero lines.

   (b) After all guns lay off the "angle of switch" from their zero lines.

   (The guns are still on parallel lines of fire.)

   (c) After distribution of fire along :—

      (i.) A frontal target.

      (ii.) An oblique target.

To obtain the distribution angle.

  Case I.

  Frontal barrage.—Where the angle HAB is between 80 deg. and 100 deg.

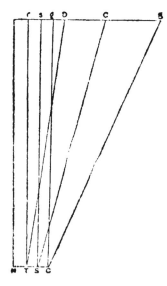

Fig. V. (not to scale).

The figure shews the guns of a 4-gun battery.

  (a) On parallel lines before distribution.

  (b) After distribution on the target AB.

Rule I.

  1. Subtract the frontage of the battery from the line to be fired on.

  (Since GH = Ag, this gives the length gB.)

  2. Find from the graph, Appendix V., graph No. 2, what angle this length subtends at the range HA.

  (Since HA = gG, this gives the angle BGg.)

  3. Divide this angle by the number of gun intervals. The angle obtained is the distribution angle of the Battery.

  (See *para. 2 above.*)

If no graph is available the angle BGg can be obtained :—

    (i.) By using the " angle of sight " formula.

$$\frac{V.I.}{H.E.} \times 3400 = \text{angle in minutes.}$$

Where V.I. = AB − GH = gB.

      H.E. = Range HA = gG.

NOTE.—This formula should not be used if the angle BGg exceeds 10 deg.

Fig. VI.

    (ii.) By measurement with a protractor. *No* lines need necessarily be drawn, but errors are easily made in measuring the angle BGg.

Example:—A battery of 8 guns, 10 yards apart, engages a target 320 yards long at a range of 2,100 yards. To find the angle of distribution to order :—

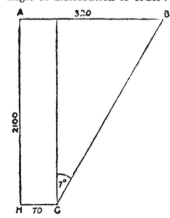

Applying Rule I.

1.   AB = 320
       GH = 70
      ————————
    AB − GH = 250

2.   Using graph, 250 yards at 2,100 yards subtends an angle of 6° 50′.

3.   Dividing 6° 50′ by 7 (since there are 7 gun intervals) = 59′.

Therefore, order 1°, as the angle is taken to the nearest 10′.

Fig. VII.   (Not to scale.)

NOTE.—(i.) **As the angle HAB is between 80° and 100°, this is a frontal barrage.**

(ii.) On the order being given:—"Distribute 1°."

No. 1 of No. 8 gun repeats "Distribute 1°."
No. 1 of No. 7   ,,   ,,   "1° right, distribute 1°,"
No. 1 of No. 6   ,,   ,,   "2° right, distribute 1°,"
No. 1 of No. 5   ,,   ,,   "3° right, distribute 1°,"
etc.   (*See* Barrage Drill, Third stage.)

Case II.

Oblique barrage.—Where angle HAB is not between 80 deg. and 100 deg.

(NOTE.—Enfilade barrage is only a type of this.)

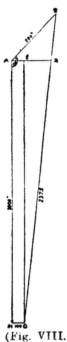

The figure shows:—

(*a*) The parallel lines of fire of the flank guns of a battery before distribution.

(*b*) The lines of fire of the flank guns after distribution on an oblique target.

It is obvious that if Rule I. is applied, the distribution would be inaccurate owing to the foreshortening of the target when viewed from the battery.   To overcome this apply Rule II.

Rule II.   Draw AX at right angles to HA. This is called the " working base," and is used instead of AB to determine the angle of distribution.

To find AX:—

(*a*) *Measure it from the map by drawing,* or,

(*b*) *Without drawing, use graph No. 2, Appendix V. to find AX.*

(*c*) *Proceed now as in Rule I., using AX instead of AB from which to subtract the battery frontage.*

(Fig. VIII.
to scale).

Noте.—As the ranges HA and GB are different, combined sights are used.

Example:—An 8-gun battery on a front of 100 yards, engages a target 500 yards long, where the angle HAB = 135 deg. and the range HA = 2,000 yards. (*See* Fig. VIII.)

To find the angle of distribution.—Apply Rule II.

By drawing, the working base AX = 320 yards.

By calculation:—

Using graph No. 2.

Since the angle HAB = 135°, then from the scale for converting oblique to equivalent frontal targets

$$AX = \cdot64 \times AB$$
$$= \cdot64 \times 500$$
$$= 320 \text{ yards.}$$

Proceeding now as in Rule I. and using AX instead of AB,

(i.)   AX = 320
            GH = 100
∴ AX − GH = 220.

(ii.) 220 yards and 2,000 yards subtends 380'

(iii.) dividing 380' by 7 (as there are 7 gun intervals) = 54' *i.e.* Order " Distribute 50'."

To find elevation.

Range GB = 2,375.   QE = 390'
Range HA = 2,000.   QE = 256'

Therefore, difference   = 134'.
             Dividing by 7 (*i.e.,* the number of gun intervals)
             Result = 19'.
             Take 20', being to the nearest 10', and order "Elevation 4° 20', 20' differences."

3. CONCENTRATION OF FIRE.

Where the frontage of the target as viewed from the battery is less than that of the battery, it is necessary to concentrate the fire of the battery from their parallel lines.

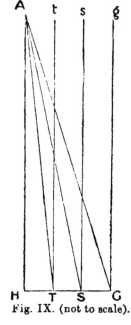

Fig. IX. (not to scale).

This figure shows the lines of fire of a 4-gun battery.

(*a*) On their zero lines.

(*b*) After concentration on the target A.

The angle tTA is the angle of concentration of the battery for the target A.

The angle sSA = twice the angle tTA.

The angle gGA = three times the angle tTA.

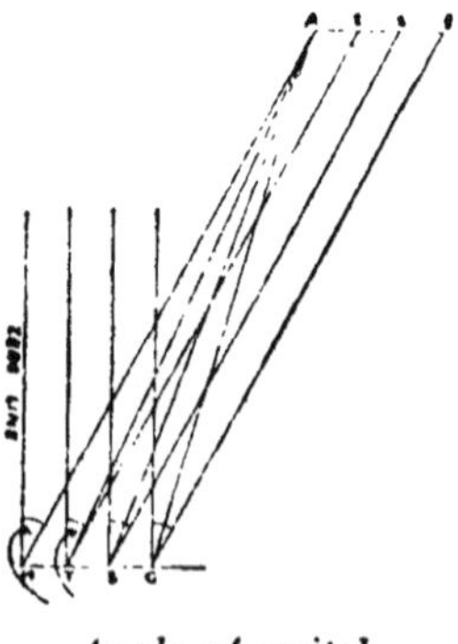

Angle of switch.
Fig. X. (not to scale).

This figure shows the lines of a 4-gun battery.

(*a*) On their zero lines.

(*b*) After all guns lay off the "angle of switch" from their zero lines.

(*See* para. 2, Figs. III. and IV.)

(*c*) After concentration on to the target A.

The angle tTA is the angle of concentration of the battery for the target A.

The angle sSA = twice the angle tTA.

The angle gGA = three times the angle tTA.

To find the angle of concentration.

Rule III.

Subtract the frontage of the target from the frontage of the battery, and proceed exactly as in Rule I., but substitute concentration for distribution.

Example :—A battery of 8 guns on a frontage of 120 yards desires to engage a target whose frontage is 40 yards, at a range of 2,100 yards. To find the angle of concentration.

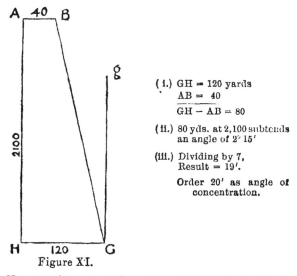

(i.) GH = 120 yards
    AB = 40
    ——————————
    GH − AB = 80

(ii.) 80 yds. at 2,100 subtends an angle of 2° 15′

(iii.) Dividing by 7,
    Result = 19′.

    Order 20′ as angle of concentration.

Figure XI.

NOTE 1.—On order being given, " Concentrate 20 min.,"

No. 1 of No. 8 gun repeats, " Concentrate 20′."
No. 1 of No. 7   ,,   " 20′ left, concentrate 20′,"
No. 1 of No. 6   ,,   " 40′   ,,   ,,   20′,"
No. 1 of No. 5   ,,   " 1°   ,,   ,,   20′,"
etc. (*See* Barrage Drill, Third stage.)

NOTE 2.—It will often be found that for flank barrages the working base, as found by the use of Rule II., will be less than the battery front, and it will then be necessary to use Rule III., and concentrate the fire.

67

NOTE 3.—*It will generally be sufficient, in order to engage a target such as an enemy concentration, to switch the fire of the battery on parallel lines without concentration or distribution of fire.*

Example:—Shewing distribution of fire along a target, after a switch.

A battery of eight guns on a frontage of 100 yards is ordered to engage a target 370 yards long at 2,200 yards range.

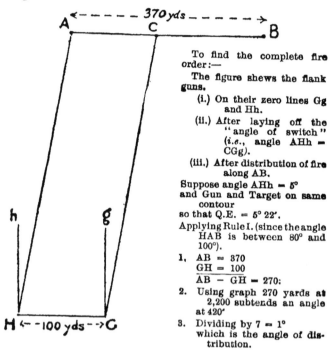

To find the complete fire order:—

The figure shews the flank guns.

(i.) On their zero lines Gg and Hh.

(ii.) After laying off the "angle of switch" (*i.e.*, angle AHh = CGg).

(iii.) After distribution of fire along AB.

Suppose angle AHh = 5° and Gun and Target on same contour so that Q.E. = 5° 22'.

Applying Rule I. (since the angle HAB is between 80° and 100°).

1. AB = 370
   GH = 100
   AB − GH = 270:

2. Using graph 270 yards at 2,200 subtends an angle at 420'

3. Dividing by 7 = 1° which is the angle of distribution.

The complete orders by the Battery Commander would be:—
        Stand to.
        All guns on zero.

All guns 5 deg. right.

No. 8 gun directs.

Distribute 1 deg.

Load.

Elevation 5 deg. 22 min.

Medium rate (or whatever rate is ordered).

Fire.

If this target formed part of a previously arranged barrage, the Battery Commander would place the results of his calculations in the Battery Chart as follows (*see* Appendix VI., No. 2) :—

No. of Barrage.	Angle of Switch.			Distribution angle.			Range.	V.I.	Q.E.
A.	5° R.			1°			2,200	0	5° 22'
A.	8	7	6	5	4	3	2	1	
	5° R	6° R	7° R	8° R	9° R	10° R	11° R	12° R	

The lower part of the Battery Chart shows the *angle of deviation* of each gun from its zero line. This is found by combining the angle of switch with the distribution angle or the necessary multiple of the distribution angle.

It will be noticed that the angle of deviation of the directing gun equals the angle of switch.

From this part of the table the gun charts are compiled.

NOTE.—(i.) Where the situation does not permit the passing of orders, the Battery Commander will employ the most suitable means of conveying the fire orders to his guns, *e.g.*, by giving orders himself to each gun Commander in turn, or sending the orders by runner to the gun Commanders.

NOTE.—Appendix VI., No. 2 and No. 3, should be read before proceeding to Section 10, para. 4.

Sec. 10.

Frontage of battery.

Definition.

The frontage of a battery is the perpendicular distance between the parallel lines of the flank guns.

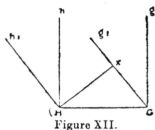

Figure XII.

The figure shows:—
1. Zero lines of flank guns of a battery, Hh and Gg.

As the angle hHG = 90 deg., the frontage of the battery = GH.

2. Parallel lines Hh₁ and Gg₁ after a switch.

The frontage o f t h e battery is now HX, *not* GH.

This is only equal to the distance between the guns when the angle (hHG) between the line of fire of the directing gun and the line of guns is a right angle.

The error arising from considering the battery frontage as the distance between the guns may be always neglected where the angle hHG is between 110 deg. and 70 deg.

In other cases greater accuracy will be ensured if the frontage HX is used rather than the distance between the guns GH.

To obtain HX:—

(a) Measure it on the map,

or (b) Use graph No. 2, Appendix V. (*See* above, Case II., Oblique Barrage.)

4. TO OBTAIN PARALLEL LINES OF FIRE.

(a) *It is very important that the lines of fire of the guns of a battery should be parallel when first laid out, and every effort should be made to attain this object.* The battery commander will then have a definite condition from which to make his calculations, and can switch his guns from one target to another without losing parallelism, distribute his fire correctly over a given front, or concentrate it on a given point, by means of the methods given above in para. 2 and para. 3. Any of the methods given below may be used, and the battery commander will choose that most suited to the situation. In general, the method depending on the distant R.O. is the quickest and most accurate, the compass the slowest and most inaccurate.

(b) Methods depending on use of compass.

Each gun is laid on the same bearing by compass. This bearing is the bearing of the zero line. The methods can be any of those given in Sec. 9.

The lines of a battery may be laid by compass when the ground renders it impossible to place the guns approximately in a line and there is no R.O. at a great distance.

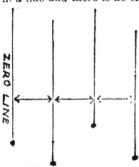

The figure shows a four-gun battery in shell holes with parallel zero lines of fire.

Figure XIII.

This may occur after the forward move of batteries to new shell hole positions, from which to create a S.O.S. barrage line. When firing in this direction the gun intervals should be as nearly equal as possible.

(c) Methods depending on the use of a director or a gun used as a director.

The zero line of the directing gun is laid out by any of the methods described in Sec. 9 and is marked by two posts.

The director is now placed in line with the two aiming posts at least 50 yards in front or rear of the battery, with the foresight towards the target and clamped at zero.

If a gun is being used the reading on the traversing dial is noted

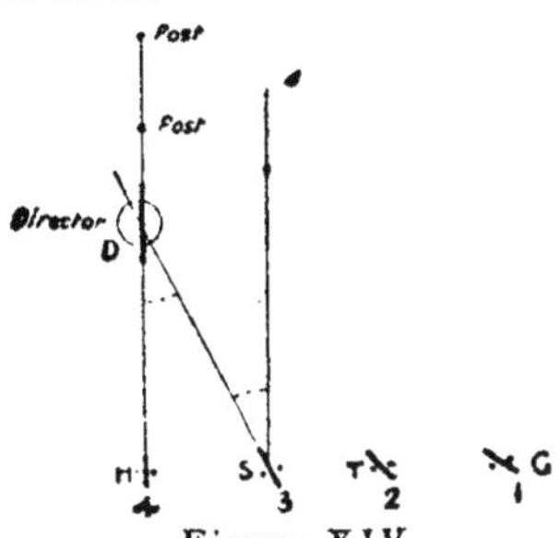

The figure shows : — The director—

(i.) In line with the two aiming posts ;

(ii.) Laid back on No. 4 gun ;

(iii.) Laid back on No. 3 gun ;

(iv.) No. 3 gun lays off the angle sSD = angle HDS. and is now on its zero line.

71

Figure XIV.

Sec. 10.

All guns now lay on the director.

The controlling officer now faces the battery and lays back over the director (*foresight* over *backsight*) on to each gun in turn.

The angles swung through are noted and given to the guns. Each gun lays off the angle given to it, and an aiming post is put out. The guns are now in parallel zero lines.

Where the director is behind the battery, the procedure is the same, except:—

      (i.) Guns are laid back on the director from *foresight* to *backsight*.

      (ii.) Director is laid on guns from backsight to foresight.

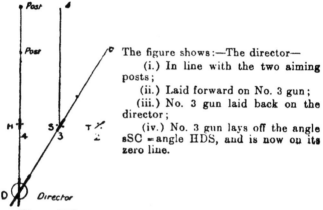

The figure shows:—The director—

      (i.) In line with the two aiming posts;

      (ii.) Laid forward on No. 3 gun;

      (iii.) No. 3 gun laid back on the director;

      (iv.) No. 3 gun lays off the angle sSC = angle HDS, and is now on its zero line.

Figure XV.

The lines of a battery may be laid in this way when the ground renders it impossible to place the guns approximately in a straight line and there is no R.O. at a great distance.

(d) *Methods depending on the use of a R.O., either on the map or put out.*

When all the guns of the same battery are laid off the same angle from the same R.O., the lines of fire will not be parallel unless:—

      (i.) The R.O. is at an infinite distance.

      (ii.) The R.O. is in direct prolongation of the line of the guns.

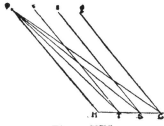

The figure shews the guns of a 4-gun battery :—

(*a*) Laid on the R.O. at P.

(*b*) After distribution to obtain parallelism.

Figure XVI.

The angle of distribution for the battery = angle tTP = angle HPT.

The angle sSP = twice angle tTP.

It also = angle HPs = twice angle HPT.

The angle gGP = three times angle tTP.

It also = angle HPG = three times angle HPT.

To obtain the distribution angle, measure the angle HPG and divide it by the number of gun intervals.

This is done by ordering flank guns to lay on each other and on R.O.; each gun notes the angle swung through. This measures angle PHG and PGH.

Add these angles together and subtract their sum from 180 deg. The result is angle HPG. Divide this angle by the number of gun intervals and this is the angle of distribution to obtain parallelism.

NOTE.—The three angles of a triangle added together = 180 deg.

> *Example.*—Angle PHG = 120°
> Angle PGH = 57°
> adding = 177°
> 180° − 177° = 3°
> Dividing by number of gun intervals (3)
> Result = 1°.

As the zero lines are unlikely to be the lines obtained above, it will be necessary to switch the parallel lines once these are obtained. In practice it is found better to order the switch angle first and the distribution angle for parallelism second. (*See* Barrage Drill, Stage 2.)

The result obtained is the same and the angle of distribution for parallelism is independent of the switch angle.

Sec. 10.

Case I.—R.O. in front of guns.

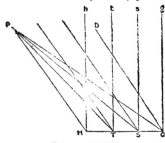

Figure XVII.

Draw GD parallel to HP.

The figure shews the lines of fire of a 4-gun battery.

(*a*). Laid on R.O. at P.

(*b*) On parallel lines after distribution.

(*c*) On parallel zero lines.

Then in order for the gun at G to fire on its zero line Gg, it must lay off the angle gGP = angle gGD plus angle DGP
= angle hHP plus angle HPG
= switch angle plus angle HPG.

Therefore, measure angle HPG as described above and divide this angle by the number of gun intervals. This is the angle of distribution for the battery.

> *Example :*—If switch angle = 60°,
> Angle of distribution = 1°.
> Order—All guns on R.O.
> All guns 60° right,
> No. 4 gun directs,
> Distribute 1°.

Case II.—R.O. behind guns.

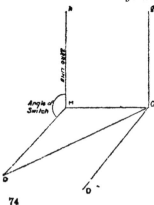

Figure XVIII.

The figure shows the flank guns of a battery :—

(*a*) Laid on R.O. ;

(*b*) On parallel zero lines.

Draw GD parallel to HP. Since Hh and Gg are parallel, and HP and GD are parallel, therefore angle hHP = angle gGD, and angle HPG = angle PGD.

Now the gun at G lays off the angle gGP

$$= \text{angle } gGD - \text{angle } PGD$$
$$= \text{angle } hHP - \text{angle } HPG.$$

Therefore, proceed as in Case I., order all guns to lay off the switch angle and *concentrate* instead of distribute.

NOTE.—The angle of concentration is obtained by dividing the angle HPG by the number of gun intervals.

It may happen that no suitable R.O. exists which is marked on the map, but some object may be used which is not on the map, and by taking a bearing to this the angle of switch necessary to obtain the zero line can be obtained.

This object can then be used to obtain parallelism as described above.

The R.O. must be as far away as possible, and it is sufficient if the guns are approximately in line.

If there is no suitable R.O. one must be put out in the line of the guns at a distance of at least 400 yards if possible; and the guns should be in line as accurately as possible.

Here the bearing to the R.O. is taken from position of the directing gun.

It may happen that the R.O. is invisible from one of the gun positions or that the gun is out of line.

In this case its line can be laid :—

    (*a*) By compass;

    (*b*) By laying on any gun which has obtained its zero line.

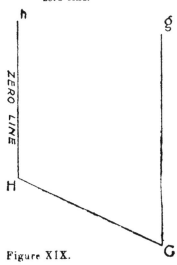

The figure shews Hh the zero line of a gun already obtained, Gg the zero line of a gun obtained as follows :—

The guns lay on each other.

The gun at H records the angle hHG.

The gun at G subtracts this from 180 deg., and lays off the result from the gun at H. It is now on the parallel line Gg.

75

Figure XIX.

NOTE.—Since Hh and Gg are parallel, angle hĤG plus angle gĜH =180 deg.

5.   INDIRECT FIRE BY MACHINE GUN BATTERIES WHERE A 1/20,000 OR LARGER SCALE MAP IS NOT AVAILABLE.

In order to deal with the tactical situation discussed in Section 40, Part I. (Open Warfare), provision must be made in the training of Machine Gun Units for applying the indirect fire of batteries without the use of contoured maps.

The principles of distribution and concentration of fire from parallel lines and the methods of obtaining parallel lines remain unchanged, but modifications are required in the method of laying out the zero line of the directing gun and obtaining its elevation.

In the following the word " director " will be taken to mean either a " director " proper or some means of improvising a director, *e.g.*, a machine gun, a compass in conjunction with an angle of sight instrument, or a sextant.

Two cases now arise :—

Case I.

Where the target can be seen from the vicinity of the battery position.

The line to the target is marked by two aiming posts.

The director is then placed in line with the two aiming posts at least 50 yards in front of, or rear of, the line of the battery, and the guns are laid for direction as described in Sec. 10, 4, c.

Elevation is obtained as in Sec. 9, para. 2, B.

Case II.

Where the target can only be observed from some distance to a flank.

The line of fire of the directing gun :—

> (i.) Is laid out by the method described in 53, B.
>
> (ii.) The battery commander orders :—
>
>> All guns parallel to No. .... gun.
>> (This being directing gun.)
>> This is done by one of the methods described in Sec. 10, para. 4.

In either case the battery commander is now in a position to distribute or concentrate his fire as occasion arises.

This type of fire should not be carried out over the heads of troops in the open, unless they are moving to a definite time table, and the clearances can be found. Sec. 12, para. 2, B.

11.—MAINTAINING LAYING.

After a gun has been laid for direction and elevation by any of the means described in Secs. 9 and 10, an aiming post is put out in order to maintain direction and elevation. The tangent sight slide is run up until the sights are aligned on the bull on the aiming post, and the laying is maintained by relaying on the bull between bursts. In addition, the elevation should be frequently checked by the clinometer. Appendix X. describes two types of aiming posts in use.

Inaccurate laying on the auxiliary aiming mark can only be avoided by training the personnel. Too much stress cannot be laid on this part of the machine gunner's training, as failure to realise the importance of accurate aiming may lead to fire becoming dangerous to our own troops, and a consequent loss of confidence by the infantry.

Machine gunners should be tested in aiming from time to time by the " triangle of error " method.

NOTE.—Where no form of artificial aiming mark is available, some natural object on the ground may be selected. This should only be regarded as a makeshift, and not taught as a general practice.

12.—SAFETY CLEARANCES.

The clearance at any point over which fire is being directed is the vertical distance of the centre of the cone above that point.

1. When indirect fire is carried out over the heads of our own troops the following rules must be adhered to in order to ensure the safety of the troops:—

(i.) The following minimum clearances of the centre of the cone are required:—

Range to Friendly Troops				Minimum Clearance	
				Yards	Metres
600 yards and under			...	11	10
700 yards	...	...	...	13	12
800	...	...	...	15	14
900	...	...	...	17	16
1,000	...	...	...	20	18
1,100	...	...	...	23	21
1,200	...	...	...	27	25
1,300	...	...	...	31	28
1,400	...	...	...	35	32
1,500	...	...	...	40	37
1,600	...	...	...	46	42
1,700	...	...	...	53	48
1,800	...	...	...	60	55
1,900	...	...	...	69	63
2,000	...	...	...	80	73

(ii.) Our own troops must not be more than 2,000 yards from the guns.

(iii.) Steps must be taken to prevent such extremes of traversing and searching as would violate (i.). This is best done by using traversing and elevating stops.

(iv.) Calculations must be carefully checked and atmospheric conditions allowed for.

(v.) The rigidity of the firing platform is essential. This is obtained by the use of the " T " base.

(vi.) Elevation must be frequently checked by the clinometer.

(vii.) The personnel must be highly trained in accurate aiming and relaying.

(viii.) The maps used must be accurate and the scale not smaller than 1/20,000.

(ix.) Worn barrels and tripods should not be used.

(x.) Our own troops should be warned when firing is going to take place.

(xi.) Clinometers should be frequently tested.

The following table shows the various causes which may result in fire becoming dangerous, and how these causes may be avoided:—

Cause	How avoided
(i.) Worn barrels.	Replacement by new barrels, but the life of a barrel is increased by care in oiling and pulling through.
(ii.) Worn mountings.	Replacement by new tripods or by the use of washers.
(iii.) Bad holding.	Training of personnel.
(iv.) Bad laying on auxiliary aiming mark.	Training of personnel.
(v.) Extremes of traversing and searching.	Training of personnel and use of traversing and depression stops.
(vi.) Error in calculation.	Practice in the use of the Tables and Graph.
(vii.) Failure to allow for atmospheric conditions.	
(viii.) Inaccurate Clinometer.	Constant testing.
(ix.) Mounting sinking.	Use of " T " bases and care in construction of firing platforms.

The importance of the rigid platform may be better realised if it is remembered that a change of elevation of 30 min. is caused if the front legs sink 1/3rd inch while the rear legs remain fixed, and *vice versa* if the rear legs sink while the front legs remain fixed. As this error is neutralized by relaying on an auxiliary aiming mark, the necessity for constant and accurate relaying is again emphasized.

NOTE.—The safety clearances are based on:—

(i.) A possibility of 5 per cent. error in range on the map.

(ii.) A possibility of 10 per cent. error in range, due to worn barrel, bad holding, etc.

(iii.) A possible error of 40 min. in the play of the tripod.

(iv.) Allowance for the lowest shot of the cone.

2. (A) To find the clearance over the friendly troops, using Tables 2 (A) or 2 (B) (Appendix IV.).

Definition of equivalent range.

The range at which the centre of the cone would strike the horizontal plane through the gun position.

It is found by using Table 1, Columns 1 and 2, and is used to determine the heights of the trajectories above the horizontal plane by means of Table 2 (A).

NOTE.—There is no equivalent range if the Q.E. is negative.

Example 1.　　　　　　　　　Target above gun.

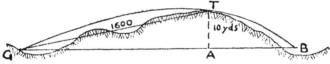

The figure shows the trajectory to hit the target at T and GB, the equivalent range on the horizontal plane through the gun position.

If GT = 1,600 yards
and target is 10 yards *above* gun.
Table 3 (A) gives QE = 177'.
Table 1, Columns 1 and 2 shew equivalent range = 1,700
i.e., GB = 1,700.

Example 2.

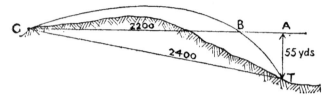

Target below gun.

The figure shows the trajectory to hit the target at **T** and GB, the equivalent range on the horizontal plane through the gun position.

> If GT = 2400 yards
> and target is 55 yards *below* gun
> Table 3 (B) gives Q.E. = 322'
> Table 1, Columns 1 and 2 shew equivalent range = 2200
>   *i.e.*, GB = 2200.

Procedure to find clearance.

Determine Q.E. and, when possible, the equivalent range.
Note the gun contour.
Note the friendly troops contour.
And so obtain the V.I. between the gun and our own troops.

The following two cases may arise : —

Case 1.

Where the trajectory, as it passes over our own troops, is *above* the horizontal plane through the gun position.

Rule.

Find the height of the trajectory at the range to our own troops above the horizontal plane through the gun position.

(This is done by finding the equivalent range and using Table 2 (A).)

If the friendly troops are above the gun, *subtract* the V.I. between the gun and our own troops from the trajectory height.

The result is the clearance. (*See* Fig. I.)

If our own troops are below the gun, *add* the V.I. to the trajectory height.

The result is the clearance. (*See* Fig. II.)

Fig. I.   *Sec. 19.*

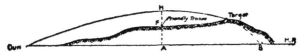

HA = height of trajectory above HP.
FA = V.I. between our own troops and gun.
Clearance = HA − FA.
        = HA − VI.

Fig. II.

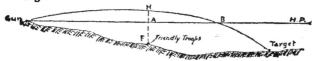

HA = height of trajectory above HP.
FA = V.I. between our own troops and gun.
Clearance = HA + FA.
        = HA + VI.

Case II.

Where the trajectory as it passes over our own troops is *below* the horizontal plane through the gun position.

Rule.

Find the depth of the trajectory at the range to our own troops below the horizontal plane through the gun position.

(This is done by finding the equivalent range and using Table 2 (A) if the Q.E. is positive, by using Table 2 (B) if the Q.E. is negative.)

Subtract the depth of the trajectory from the V.I. between the gun and our own troops.

The result is the clearance. (*See* Fig. I. and Fig. II.)

HA = Depth of trajectory below HP.
FA = V.I. between our own troops and guns.
Clearance = V.I. − HA.

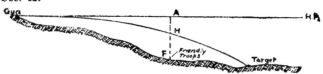

HA = Depth of trajectory below HP.
FA = V.I. between our own troops and guns.
Clearance = V.I. − HA.

Clearances may also be found by using graph No. 1. (*See* Appendix V.)

This method is much shorter and mistakes are less liable to be made.

(B) Where fire is being carried out as described in Sec. 9, para. 2 B, clearances can be found as follows:—

(i.) Determine the range to our own troops and the angle of sight from the gun to our own troops in exactly the same manner as determining the range to the target and the angle of sight to the target.

(ii.) Obtain the V.I. between the gun and our own troops from the formula:—

$$V.I. = \frac{(\text{Angle of sight from gun to our own troops}) \times (\text{Range from gun to our own troops})}{8,400.}$$

It is now simple to find the clearance proceeding, as described in 2 (A) above.

3. CLEARING THE OBSTRUCTION.

In all cases where an obstruction exists between the gun and the target, it is necessary to ensure that the shots will clear the obstruction before opening fire.

To do this:—

1. After the gun has been laid for direction and elevation adjust the tangent sight slide to read the range from the gun to the top of the obstruction. If on looking along the sights the obstruction is not visible, the shots will clear.

NOTE.—If the line of sight only just clears the obstruction, the lower half of the cone will strike the obstruction.

2. If the distance to the obstruction is under 100 yards put the sights at zero (the gun being already laid for direction and elevation); if, on looking along the sights the obstruction is not visible, the shots will clear.

3. If the obstruction is invisible (such as the summit of a hill hidden by a false crest) neither of the methods given above will apply, and the clearance must be found by the method given in para. 1, substituting "Obstruction" for "Our Own Troops." The clearance must be at least equal to half the height of the cone.

*4. TRAJECTORY TABLES.

Table 2 (A) is the trajectory table for positive quadrant elevations. It is compiled as follows:—

To find the height of the trajectory at a distance GB when firing at a range GT.

By definition angle TGC = TE for range GT, Sec. 49, para. 1, and assuming the rigidity of the trajectory,

By definition angle AGC = TE for range GA
= TE for range GB.

(since GA = GB approximately the angle AGB being small).

But angle BGA = angle TGC − angle AGC
= TE for range GT − TE for range GB.

Now applying the angle of sight formula

$$S = \frac{VI}{HE} \times 3438 \text{ and so } VI = \frac{S \times HE}{3438}$$

and remembering S = angle BGA. Sec. 49, para. 3.

$$VI = AB$$
$$HE = GB$$

the clearance $AB = \dfrac{(TE \text{ for range } GT - TE \text{ for range } GB) \times GB}{3438}$

Example:—To find height of 1,700 yards trajectory at 1,000 yards.

TE for 1700 = 177
TE for 1000 = 62
$$AB = \frac{(177 - 62) \times 1000}{3438}$$
$$= \frac{115 \times 1000}{3438}$$
$$= 33\cdot4 \text{ yards.}$$

Table 2 (A) gives 33·3.

Table 2 (B) is the trajectory table for negative quadrant elevations. It is compiled as follows:—

Horizontal plane.

To find the depth of the trajectory below the horizontal plane through the gun position at a distance GB when firing with a quadrant elevation = angle BGC.

By definition angle BGC = QE

,,   ,,   ,,   AGC = TE for range GA

= TE for range GB

(since GA = GB approximately)

But angle BGA = angle BGC + angle AGC

Now applying the angle of slight formula

$$S = \frac{V.I.}{H.E.} \times 3438$$

and remembering S = angle BGA

V.I. = AB

H.E. = GB

$$\text{Then } AB = \frac{(QE + TE \text{ for range GB}) \times GB}{3438}$$

Example:—Supposing a negative angle of Q.E. of 100 min.

To find depth of trajectory below horizontal plane at a distance of 1,000 yards.

Then TE for 1000 yards = 62'.

$$AB = \frac{(100' - 62') \times 1000}{3438}$$

= 47·1 yards.

Table 23 (B) gives 47·2.

In addition, all graphs and other aids to determine clearances without calculation are based on these Trajectory Tables.

13.—NIGHT FIRING.

1. When indirect fire is carried out by night, the gun position must be fixed by day, and a post at some known direction from the gun position must be placed in the ground

by day, or at dawn or dusk, as it is usually impossible to do these things with accuracy after dark. After dark, the post must be replaced by some illuminated aiming mark.

2. *Night Aiming Mark.*—(a) Experiments with aiming marks covered with luminous paint have not proved successful. Even on a dark night such aiming marks require very frequent exposure to artificial light in order to retain the necessary luminosity, and even then afford no *definite* point of aim.

Another objection is that such aiming marks cannot be seen at all in the " half-light " of dawn or dusk, or on a moonlight night.

(b) Lamps containing oil burners or candles are a constant source of trouble because the lamp must be lighted before, and extinguished after each target is engaged. If this is not done the mark becomes obscured by the smoke of combustion, and in the case of a candle the lamp becomes hot and the candle melts.

(c) The most satisfactory aiming mark is an electric box as described in Appendix X.

The light can be switched on from the gun position and can be put out as soon as the firing is completed. The box is easily carried and is not likely to break during transport.

The aiming mark is 12 inches wide, and therefore, when placed 9½ yards from the gun, gives a traverse of 2 degrees. This is a great advantage over " point " aiming marks, where the limit of traverse has to be guessed.

With this aiming box, used in conjunction with the luminous bar foresight (Appendix X.) and a luminous backsight, any type of indirect fire, including barrage fire, can be performed by night with accuracy.

3. *An Electric Torch* is essential at the gun for reading graduations on the Direction Dial and tangent sight, and for setting the clinometer.

4. *Depression Stops* and *Traversing Stops*, when set correctly, automatically ensure the safety of our own Infantry, and thus diminish the strain on the firer.

5. *Flash Obscurers* have been produced which effectively conceal the flash from view, but they invariably disperse the cone to such an extent that they make overhead fire impossible. Consequently, there is no pattern which can be recommended.

85

On the other hand, it has been proved experimentally that screens of canvas or sandbags have no effect on a cone which

 is fired through them, and such screens when wet effectively screen the flash. Care should be taken to screen the flash at the sides as well as the front.

6. When the firing is done from positions some way behind our front line, and especially when this is reached by overland routes, special precautions must be taken against endangering friendly troops who are passing near the gun position.

This is done by posting sentries or by wiring in the danger area. The safety of working parties and patrols in No Man's Land must be secured by liaison with Battalions.

14.—SEARCHING REVERSE SLOPES.

In order to search a reverse slope effectively, the gun must be placed at such a distance from the crest that the fall of the bullet is steeper than the slope of the ground.

Table 7 (Appendix IV.) has been compiled to enable the machine gunner to do this without making elaborate calculations. If this Table be used according to the following instructions, the angle ABC (*see* diagram above) will be between 100 and 200 minutes.

1. METHOD OF USING TABLE 7.

(i.) Find the fall in yards, per 100 yards of the slope. To do this it is best to find the fall for several hundred yards of the slope, and then calculate the average fall per hundred yards.

(Suppose the fall is 6 yards per 100 yards.)

(ii.) Draw a line on the map representing the probable line of fire. This will be so as to engage the target in enfilade when possible.

(iii.) Observe from the map, whether the gun is likely to be above or below the top of the slope.

(iv.) Suppose it is above. On the right half of Table 7 (Gun above Crest) and in the top column find the figure 6, and notice the range in the column beneath it (*i.e.*, 1,400 yards).

(v.) Measure back from the top of the slope 1,400 yards along the line of fire.

(vi.) Find the difference between the height of this point and the height of the top of the slope (say 20 yards).

(vii.) Find 20 in the centre column, and, reading along the column to the right, find the range below the 6 in the top column (*i.e.*, 1,600 yards).

(viii.) Measure back 1,600 yards from the top of the slope, along the line of fire. The point thus found is the point in which to place the gun.

(ix.) Knowing the gun position, and the position and height of the top of the slope, find by the ordinary methods of indirect fire, the direction and elevation necessary to hit the top of the slope.

2. SPECIAL POINTS.

(i.) In certain cases both sides of Table 7 may be satisfied.

Example:—

Fall 5 yards per 100 yards.

Then using the right side of Table 7, the gun must be placed 1,350 yards from the slope, when the gun is above the crest. Or, using left side, if the range is 1,850 yards, the gun must be below the crest.

In such a case the controller can decide for himself which position is the best to occupy.

(ii.) Neither side of Table 7 may be satisfied.

Example:—

Fall 5 yards per 100 yards.

On measuring back 1,350 yards, the gun may be *below* the crest, and in measuring back 1,850 yards, the gun may be *above* the crest. In such a case, which will be extremely rare, choose a position between the two which is on the same level as the crest. The reverse slope can be engaged from this position.

(iii.) As the searching of reverse slopes is just a special type of indirect fire, searching and traversing will be employed as usual, with the exception that searching will be very restrained.

If AB represents the length of the beaten zone on the horizontal plane, AC will represent the length of beaten zone

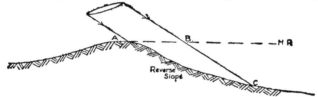

on the slope AC. In all cases AC will greatly exceed AB, and consequently two or three turns of the elevating wheel will cover a target several hundreds of yards in length.

(iv.) The final position indicated by Table 7 may be an impossible one, say, in a river or a marsh. In such a case a gun position should be selected further away from the slope rather than nearer to the slope.

By moving further back the range is increased, and consequently the angle of descent of the bullet, but by going nearer to the crest the angle of descent is decreased, and it may become impossible to search the reverse slope at all.

(v.) Fire should be directed at the top of the target, which may, or may not, be the crest of the hill. If the top of the target is not the top of the hill, calculations should be made to see if the hill will be cleared or not. If the crest is not cleared, the gun should be taken back to such a range that the obstruction will be cleared.

(See example map attached.)

Search the track from Q.11.d.4615 to Q.11.d.3951.

Length of road = 200 yards. Fall is 10 metres = 11 yards. Therefore fall per 100 yards = 5½ yards. Work on 6 yards. The gun will be below the crest, so use left side of Table 7,

Measure back 1,850 yards (*i.e.*, Q.24.c.22.51). Height of this position is 71 metres. Height of top of target is 110 metres. Therefore the gun is 39 metres = 43 yards below the top of the target. ⊙

Find 40 in the centre column of Table 7, and find the range opposite this and below the 6 on the left (*i.e.*, 1,800 yards). This is the final gun position (at Q.24.c.20.57). If this point is unsuitable for a gun position, move back along line of fire until a suitable position is found (say, at Q.24.c.3100) Then calculate the angle of quadrant elevation in the usual manner, and before firing ascertain whether the obstruction at Q.17.b.60.30 will be cleared.

15.—ERRORS.

The most probable errors which affect indirect laying have been described in the preceding analysis. These errors are now summarised in order to assist the Machine Gun Company Commander to draw up his training programme.

Errors on the part of Officers.

(i.) Inaccurate map work.

(ii.) Inaccurate compass work, which may affect both the fixing of the gun position and laying out the line of fire.

(iii.) Choice of reference object too near the gun position.

(iv.) Inaccurate calculations and failure to allow for atmospheric changes.

(v.) Use of instruments such as clinometers, angle of sight instruments, when not in accurate adjustment, and of worn-out material, such as barrels, etc.

Errors on part of Personnel.

(i.) Inaccurate aiming.

(ii.) Inaccurate placing of elevation on the gun.

(iii.) Inaccurate use of traversing dials, " T " aiming marks and bar foresights.

(iv.) Failure to " oil up," etc., during a barrage.

16.—MODIFICATIONS IN EQUIPMENT.

1. SAFETY DEVICES.

In order to secure the safety of the troops, over whose heads fire is being directed, it is most important to ensure the rigidity of the mounting.

Without this, traversing and depression stops do not prevent fire becoming dangerous if the mounting sinks, because these form parts of the mountings. This rigidity is obtained : —

> (i.) By careful construction of firing platforms.
>
> (ii.) By the use of " T " bases.

The latter is much preferable.

Fig. 1, Appendix IX., shows a type of " T " base easily made, but which must be adjusted to each tripod.

Fig. 2, Appendix IX., shows a type which is : —

> (i.) Collapsible and therefore more easily carried, and less likely to render the carrier conspicuous.
>
> (ii.) Adjustable.

After the tripod has been placed on the " T " base, which in soft ground should be reinforced by a layer of sandbags underneath, a few sandbags are placed across the legs.

Provided that a rigid mounting has been obtained, traversing stops prevent the firer swinging his gun beyond the prescribed limits of traverse.

At the same time depression stops prevent the fire becoming dangerous by depression of the gun.

2. In order to obtain the accuracy of direction now required for indirect fire, it is necessary to be able to lay off to 10 min. This cannot be done by the direction dial, and is done by : —

> (i.) The " T "-shaped aiming mark, Fig. I., Appendix X. : This is graduated in inches, and, when placed 9½ yards from the gun—
>
> > 1 inch represents a traverse of 10 minutes.
> > 6 inches ,, ,, ,, ,, 1 degree.

The aiming mark gives a traverse of 3 degrees either side. It cannot be used at night.

> (ii.) The combination of the bar foresight, telescopic aiming post and night-firing box, Fig. 2, Appendix X., allows : —
>
> > (a) 7 deg. either side of the centre to be laid off and readings to 10 min. intervals.
> >
> > (b) A traverse of 2 deg. either side of the centre line by placing the post 9½ yards from the gun, with arms horizontal.

(*c*) Elevation through 4 deg. if the arms are vertical.

(*c*) Elevation through 4 deg. if the arms are 1 deg. either side of centre without moving the cursor on the bar foresight, and 7 deg. to be laid off either side of the centre by moving the cursor.

3. Bayonet signalling shutters (Venetian flappers) have been often used for controlling the fire of a battery.

4. Condenser bags have been found useless, and are replaced by petrol tins.

5. The introduction of a rotatable dial much simplifies laying off angles, as it overcomes the difficulties of addition and subtraction, over which mistakes have been easily made in the past.

6. The necessity of accurate indirect fire by a large number of guns renders necessary clinometers on a scale of one per gun.

7. Some form of large protractor in the shape of a sector of a circle with an angle of 30-45 deg.

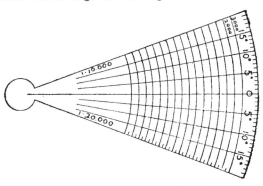

17.—MACHINE GUN BARRAGE FIRE.
(See Part I., Sec. 5 and 6.)

1. Barrage fire by machine guns is the fire of a large number of guns acting under a centralised control, directed on to definite lines or areas, in which the frontage engaged by a gun approximates 40 yards.

Barrage fire is carried out by:—

       (i.) Artillery.
       (ii.) Trench Mortars.
       (iii.) Machine Guns.

The best results in any operation can only be obtained by conceiving the barrage plan as a whole and allotting to the different weapons tasks which their characteristics render them most fitted to carry out.

There are four types of barrage fire:—

       (i.) Preliminary bombardment.
       (ii.) Creeping barrage.
       (iii.) Standing barrage.
       (iv.) Back area barrage.

2. The "harassing fire" of machine guns forms an integral part of the preliminary bombardment, and the object of the fire is to:—

       (i.) Lower efficiency of enemy working parties.
       (ii.) Increase difficulty of transport of munitions and supplies.
       (iii.) Cause deterioration of enemy morale.

This object can be obtained by engaging the following targets:—

       (*a*) Targets previously engaged by the artillery —more especially wire-entanglements and defences that have been damaged.
       (*b*) Communication trenches which can be taken in enfilade.
       (*c*) Routes, tracks taken by ration parties and reliefs, dumps, tramways, etc.
       (*d*) Certain field battery positions which may have been erected within range of machine gun fire.

By close co-operation between machine guns and other arms it is possible to drive the traffic from overland routes into the trenches, thereby causing:—

       (*a*) Congestion and delay
       (*b*) Casualties from the artillery fire on the communication trenches from their enfilade guns.

During the period more closely approaching zero day when the enemy defences have been knocked about and the morale of the garrison has been shaken, the plan of concentrating the guns of one battery on to carefully chosen centres of activity, and opening rapid fire for a short period is effective. This type of fire is known as " area shooting." This treatment should be applied to different points at irregular intervals

3. The objects of barrage fire on zero day are to : —

(*a*) Prevent the enemy manning his parapets and installing his machine guns.

(*b*) Interfere with the effective use of machine guns in rear.

(*c*) Prevent supplies of food and ammunition being brought up.

(*d*) Prevent reinforcement of the garrison.

(*e*) Destroy morale.

(*f*) Place a protective barrage at every definite stage of an advance.

(*g*) Save our own troops at all times from casualties by keeping down the fire of the enemy infantry, machine guns, etc.

By these means Infantry Battalions are enabled to : —

(*a*) Advance and seize objectives previously allotted.

(*b*) Organize for defence ground won during the delicate period when troops are suffering from nervous and physical strain, the loss of leaders and men, and the unfamiliarity of their surroundings.

These objects are obtained by creeping, standing and back area barrages carried out by the artillery, trench mortars, and machine guns in conjunction.

4. In order to enable the machine guns to carry out the *rôle* allotted to them in the barrage scheme, the machine gun barrage must fulfil the following conditions:—

(i.) It must be equally applicable to the " set piece " where the " time factor " is relatively unimportant, and to the later stages of large operations involving the forward movement of batteries to new positions from which to create a barrage, in which case the " time factor " becomes of paramount importance.

(ii.) It must apply also to conditions of semi-open and open warfare, becoming relatively more important as the troops get out of range of the bulk of their artillery.

(iii.) It must be flexible, *i.e.*, it must be possible to create a zone of intense machine gun fire on any area with accuracy and rapidity.

(iv.) It must be capable of being taught and carried out as a drill.

These conditions can only be obtained by simplicity of :—

(*a*) Organization.

(*b*) Laying.

(*c*) Fire Control.

(*d*) Drill.

5. ORGANIZATION OF GUNS FOR BARRAGE FIRE.

(*a*) Guns for barrage fire are organized into groups and batteries. The group normally consists of between 16 and 24 guns. If the group is considerably larger, it will be necessary to divide it into sub-groups, each under a sub-group commander. The group is commanded by the Group Commander, who is a Company Commander, but may be the D.M.G.O.

His normal position is at the Brigade Headquarters in whose area he is operating. He is assisted by an officer. Normally each Brigade has one group of barrage guns.

The group is divided into batteries or fire units of 4, 6 or 8 guns. The normal size of a battery is 8 guns. Each battery is commanded by an officer who is known as the Battery Commander. He is assisted by one officer per four guns and one N.C.O. to every two guns—who is not below the rank of corporal. Each gun is commanded by a N.C.O. or senior private—who is *not* the No. 1 of the gun and is known as the Gun Commander.

Batteries are lettered from the right A, B, C, etc., throughout the Corps front; in the case of a forward move these become A2, B2, C2, etc., for the first move; A3, B3, C3, etc., for the second move, and so on.

(*b*) The duties of the Group Commander are:—

(i.) To carry out the orders of the D.M.G.O.

(ii.) Organize his group into batteries.

(iii.) To make all preliminary preparations, which include estimates of S.A.A., oil, water, etc.

(iv.) To make preparation for the formation of dumps and communications.

(v.) Issue operation orders which deal with the location and tasks of each battery. The task is in the form of a table showing the times, targets, rates of fire for each lift, and any moves. These orders must be issued in ample time for the Battery Commander to make his calculations and send these to the Group Commander to check.

(vi.) To provide himself with a fighting map showing zero lines and tasks of each battery (Appendix VII., No. 1).

(c) The duties of the Battery Commander are:—

(i.) To lay out the zero lines of his battery in the position ordered by the Group Commander.

(ii.) To carry out orders of the Group Commander detailed above in (iii.), (iv.), and (v.).

(Specimen of Battery Charts, Appendix VI.)

(iii.) To issue a gun chart to each Gun Commander. (Appendix VI., No. 3.)

(iv.) To provide himself with a fighting map showing zero lines and tasks of his battery. (Appendix VII., No. 2.)

(v.) To see that every " Commander " in his battery, including himself, is provided with an understudy.

(vi.) To supervise the fire of his battery.

(d) The duties of the Gun Commander are:—

(i.) To control the fire of his gun as ordered on his gun chart.

(ii.) To control the fire as taught in " Barrage Drill."

(iii.) To see the correct elevation and direction is *placed* and *maintained* on his gun.

(iv.) To watch for signals from the officer controlling the fire.

(v.) In the event of a barrage not on the chart being ordered, to see that the correct fire order is passed down, and that his gun is correctly laid before repeating " No. — gun, ready to fire."

These duties can only be performed *in toto* when the tactical situation permits. It will often be impossible to prepare elaborate fighting maps and charts.

6. LAYING AND FIRE CONTROL.

Although machine gun barrage fire can be carried out by controlling the fire of each gun singly, experience has shown that the barrage so produced is not flexible, that calculations are laborious, and control difficult.

The introduction of the Battery System (*see* Section 10) has rendered it possible to produce a flexible barrage, easily controlled and obtained by the aid of extremely simple calculations. This is the normal method of producing machine gun barrage fire.

7. BARRAGE DRILL.

In order that a battery may work in the field with efficiency, the methods of battery fire must be learnt as a drill. This will enable the personnel in action to reproduce automatically the movements learned in practice, with such modifications as the conditions of battle may impose.

Equipment Required.

Guns and tripods.
Spare parts.
Ammunition boxes (4 per gun).
Condenser tubes and bags (or petrol tins).
" T " shaped bases.

Zero aiming posts and " T " aiming marks.
Sandbags and shovels.
Shutter for controlling fire.
Clinometers or spirit levels.
Megaphone.

First Stage.

Guns and equipment will be laid out as in elementary drill. A Gun Commander will be appointed for each gun.

(i.) " FALL IN."—Teams fall in as in elementary drill, Gun Commanders on the right of No. 1. Teams in line, dressed by the right.

(ii.) Battery Commander indicates the reference object (if one is being employed).

(iii.) " NUMBER."—As in elementary drill.

(iv.) " TAKE POST."—As in elementary drill, all numbers standing to attention.

No. 3 has with him condenser bag (or petrol tin), four boxes of ammunition and aiming post.

No. 4 has " T " shaped base and shovel. Gun Commander takes up position on left of No. 1, with cleaning rod and clinometer.

(v.) " TELL OFF BY GUNS."—Gun Commanders number off from the right:—No. 1 gun, etc.

(vi.) " PREPARE FOR BARRAGE."—No. 1 examines the tripod and No. 2 prepares the gun (condenser tube fixed) for action.

No. 3 inspects the ammunition.

No. 4 doubles forward with " T " shaped base and shovel.

Battery Commander aligns " T " shaped bases, and on the Battery Commander's signal Nos. 4 fix the bases firmly in the ground, and double to the rear.

Nos. 5 and 6 fill sandbags and prepare for belt filling, under cover.

Second Stage.

To obtain parallel zero lines in the required direction, the following is only one of several methods taught. All methods should be practised.

(vii.) " FLANK GUNS—MOUNT GUN."—The flank guns mount on the " T " shaped bases, Nos. 4, 5 and 6 bringing up sandbags, guns lay on each other, No. 2 of each gun notes reading on direction dial and signals with his hand to the other No. 2, when this is complete. Both guns now lay on R.O. and note the angle swung through. These angles are passed along to the Battery Commander, who then calculates the distribution angle to obtain parallel lines.

(viii.) " REMAINDER — MOUNT GUN."—Remaining guns mount guns on " T "-shaped bases and lay on R.O.

No. 3 of each gun brings up four boxes of ammunition and condenser bag (or petrol tin).

Nos. 4, 5 and 6 bring up sandbags.

Nos. 2 and 3 sandbag the tripod.

No. 2 fixes condenser bag (or petrol tin).

Gun Commander takes up clinometer and cleaning rod.

(ix.) " ALL GUNS—DEGREES RIGHT OR LEFT."—
(This angle will be such that it brings the zero lines of the
directing gun in the required direction.)

This order is repeated by Nos. 1 in succession from the
left, who immediately lay off the angle ordered.

Nos. 3 double forward to the gun, and pace out 9½ yards
carrying zero posts and " T " shaped aiming marks.   The
" T " aiming mark is placed as ordered by No. 1, and is held
in position by No. 3, pending the order of distribution to
obtain parallel lines.

(x.) " No. —— GUN DIRECTS."—(Normally this will be
left gun.)   This order is repeated by each No. 1.

(xi.) " DISTRIBUTE   20   min."—This   is   the   angle
obtained by the battery commander in para. 7.

The angle 20 min. has been used simply for the purpose of
illustration.   The same applies to all subsequent angles.

Then for a battery of eight guns this order would be
passed along as follows :—

> No. 1 of No. 8 gun repeats " Distribute 20 min."
> No. 3 fixes zero post and " T " aiming mark as
> ordered by No. 1.

> No. 1 of No. 7 gun repeats " 20 min. right—
> Distribute 20 min.," and lays off 20 min. right on
> " T " aiming mark.   No. 3 then fixes zero post and
> " T " aiming mark as ordered by No. 1.

> No. 1 of No. 6 gun repeats " 40 min. right—
> Distribute 20 min.," and lays off 40 min. right on
> " T " aiming mark.   No. 3 then fixes zero post and
> " T " aiming mark as ordered by No. 1—and so on for
> the remaining guns.

The guns are now laid on their parallel zero lines.

Before proceeding with the drill the Battery Commander
will order " Check zero lines," when the orders given in
9, 10 and 11 will be repeated, with the exception that the zero
posts will be left in the ground.

*These zero posts will not be moved once parallel lines
have been obtained.*

(xii.) " STAND CLEAR."—Teams fall in five yards in
rear of gun and stand at ease.

Third Stage.—Distribution and Concentration.

(xiii.) " STAND TO."—Nos. 1 and 2 take up their positions at the gun. The Gun Commander kneels down with the clinometer on the left of No. 1.

(xiv.) EXAMPLES OF DISTRIBUTION.—" All guns 6 deg. right." Each No. 1 repeats and lays off 6 deg. right from zero, using direction dial.

" No. 8 Gun Directs." ·Each No. 1 repeats.

" Distribute 1 deg. 10 min." This order is carried out as explained in 11.

(xv.) EXAMPLE OF CONCENTRATION.—" All guns 5 deg. left." Each No. 1 repeats and lays off 5 deg. left from zero, using direction dial.

" No. 8 gun directs." Each No. 1 repeats.

" Concentrate 20 min." No. 1 of No. 8 gun repeats " Concentrate 20 min."

No. 3 fixes his " T " aiming mark.

No. 1 of No. 7 gun repeats " 20 min. left—Concentrate 20 min.," and lays off 20 min. left on the " T " aiming mark. No. 3 then fixes the " T " aiming mark as ordered by No. 1.

No. 1 of No. 6 gun repeats " 40 min. left—Concentrate 20 min.," and lays off 40 min. left on " T " aiming mark. No. 3 then fixes the " T " aiming mark as ordered by No. 1— and so on.

(xvi.) " LOAD."—As in elementary drill.

(xvii.) " ELEVATION 3 deg."—Each No. 1 repeats and Gun Commander lays the gun for elevation.

No. 1 adjusts the tangent sight on the " T " shaped aiming mark, and notes the reading.

(xviii.) EXAMPLE OF COMBINED SIGHTS.—" Elevation 4 deg. 20 min.—20 min. differences." No. 1 of No. 8 gun repeats " Elevation 4 deg. 20 min.—20 min. differences."

Gun Commander sets clinometer at 4 deg. 20 min.

No. 1 of No. 7 gun repeats " Elevation 4 deg. 40 min.— 20 min. differences."

Gun Commander sets clinometer at 4 deg. 40 min.

(xix.) TRAVERSE will be 1 deg. right, 1 deg. left, unless otherwise ordered. No traverse for concentration.

(xx.) RATE OF FIRE—Slow, medium, or rapid.

(xxi.) " FIRE."—Shutter lowered.

Bursts of fire should not be less than 15-20 rounds.

No. 1 relays between bursts.

Unless concentrating tap between bursts.

Accuracy in relaying must always be insisted on.

(xxii.) " CEASE FIRE."—Shutter released.

Procedure after first lift or first belt. (Whichever is shorter.)

No. 1 unloads and clears gun.

No. 2 removes outer casing, tests muzzle cup and cleans the barrel, replaces outer casing.

No. 1 oils up, reloads and lays for direction.

Gun Commander puts on elevation.

No. 2 signals ready to fire.

Procedure after every 1,000 rounds : —

    No. 1 unloads and clears gun.

    No. 2 cleans barrel and replenishes water in barrel casing. (If necessary.)

    No. 1 oils up, reloads and lays for direction.

    Gun Commander puts on elevation.

No. 2 signals " Ready to Fire."

(xxiii.) " UNLOAD."—As in elementary drill. Gun Commander reports " No. 1 gun clear," " No. 2 gun clear," and so on.

(xxiv.) " OUT OF ACTION."—Guns dismounted at firing point.

Nos. 3, 4, 5 and 6 double forward and retire with aiming posts, belt boxes, " T " shaped bases, etc.

NOTE.—Interchange gun numbers as frequently as possible.

Fourth Stage.

(xxv.) Batteries should be practised in coming into action in different positions, obtaining parallel lines by different methods, and firing by barrage charts. In the latter case verbal orders should be dispensed with as far as possible.

(xxvi.) In the final stages of training, batteries should be practised on the ground from the map of the district, and

Group Commanders should practise the Battery Commanders in applying the fire of their batteries to any target with rapidity and accuracy.

NOTE.—In elementary stages it may be found better for the Gun Commanders to pass orders rather than the Nos. 1.

8.   RATES OF FIRE.

(i.) To prevent waste of S.A.A., to ensure time for relaying and oiling (thereby prolonging the life of the gun), and to enable estimates of S.A.A. to be made in advance, rates of fire must be laid down for rigid observance by each gun.

(ii.) Normal rates of fire are:—

(*a*) *Slow fire.*—60—75 rounds per minute fired in bursts of 15—25.

This is the rate for long period barrage fire.

(*b*) *Medium fire.*—125—150 rounds per minute. This is the rate that can be used to speed up slow fire for short periods. It can be maintained for about half-an-hour, and should not be attempted for a longer period.

(*c*) *Rapid fire.*—250—300 rounds per minute. This rate is used in response to S.O.S. calls, but should only be maintained for a few minutes, after which the fire should be reduced to medium or slow rate.

(*d*) *Harassing fire.*—1,000 rounds per hour. This may be carried out at slow, medium, or rapid rates.

(iii.) Before ordering rates of fire, the following factors must be considered:—

(*a*) Tactical requirements of the barrage.

(*b*) Frontage per gun.

Obviously it will be necessary, if the concentration of guns is thin, to fire at a more rapid rate than if the concentration is thick, in order to produce the same result.

(*c*) Time during which the barrage is to be fired.

(*d*) Number of filled belts per gun available.

(*e*) Rate at which belts can be filled.

(*f*) Wear and tear of guns.

Assuming two belt-fillers per gun, and the rate of belt-filling by hand to be:—

4 belts per man the 1st hour.

3 ,, ,, ,, ,, 2nd hour.

If 14 belts per gun are available, then

(i.) It will be possible to fire 22 belts in one hour —*i.e.*, 5,500 rounds, but this will leave all the belts empty.

(ii.) It will be possible to fire 28 belts in two hours, *i.e.*, 3,500 rounds per hour.

It is the belt problem which imposes the " Slow Rate of Fire " for all long period barrages, and it is advisable to increase the number of belts per gun for large operations.

9. LIFE OF BARRELS.

The most important factors which affect the life of a barrel are:—

(i.) The temperature of the water.

(ii.) Oiling.

(*a*) With the rate of fire approximating 1,000 rounds per hour, fired intermittently, frequent oiling of the barrel, the water below boiling point or only boiling for short periods, the life of the barrel is 20,000 to 25,000 rounds.

This corresponds to " Harassing Fire."

(*b*) With a rate of fire exceeding 3,500 rounds per hour, fired continuously, frequent oiling of the barrel, the water boiling for long periods, the life of the barrel is 12,000 to 15,000 rounds.

This corresponds to normal forms of barrage fire and S.O.S. calls.

(*c*) A failure to oil the barrel in both the above cases at regular intervals appears to decrease the life by 3,000 to 4,000 rounds.

The loss of range due to worn barrels is not at present definitely known, but experiments have shown that the lengths of the beaten zones become nearly twice those given in the tables, and that the loss apparently does not exceed 5 per cent. of the range.

18.—COMMUNICATIONS.

(See Part I., Section 29.)

1. No proper fire control is possible without a comprehensive system of telephonic communications. This necessitates the most careful co-ordination of the machine gun signalling personnel available.

SYSTEM OF COMMUNICATIONS.

2. *Offensive Operations.*

(*a*) Forward Guns.—These can communicate through the Battalion report centre, in whose area they are operating. (*See* Sec. 4, para. 12, and Sec. 29, para. 2, of Part I.)

(*b*) Rear Guns.—Appendix III., A, shows the system where one group of guns is affiliated to one Brigade; when batteries move forward they connect to the Brigade Forward Station. When the Brigade Commander moves forward to the forward station the Group Commander accompanies him, and so keeps in touch with his batteries and Forward Observation Station.

3. *Trench Warfare.*

Appendix III., B., shows system for a Division with two Brigades in the line.

Owing to the necessity for Brigade and Battalion Commanders to be able to communicate quickly with Machine Gun Company Headquarters, and the necessity of keeping messages secret, Fullerphones are required at each Machine Gun Company Headquarters. In cases where sniping batteries are employed, these must be connected by telephone to a forward observation station, from which the controlling officer sends down the necessary fire orders to engage any target he wishes.

4. *Open Warfare.*

Companies should maintain their communications with Sections by signal or wire.

Brigades will be responsible for maintaining communications with Companies.

NOTE.—Further information on this subject is given in S.S. 191, *Intercommunication in the Field.*

APPENDIX I.

ORDERS FOR GUN POSITION No..........

1. Fire is only to be opened by order of the Gun Commander unless a sudden emergency arises, in which case the sentry will use his own initiative.

2. When relieving another gun team or sentry, the following facts will always be ascertained:—

    (a) Whether the gun has been fired during the relief.

    (b) If fired, what the target was.

    (c) If fired, the emplacement from which it was fired.

    (d) Whether any instructions have been received as to friendly patrols or wiring parties.

3. The sentry will always inspect the gun when taking over the position.

4. The sentry on duty must have an accurate knowledge of the targets shown on the fighting map.

5. In case of alarm, or a gas attack, the sentry will wake the gun team.

6. The gun will be cleaned daily, and the *points before firing* gone through both morning and night. The gun must be kept free from dirt, and in the trenches may be kept wrapped up in a waterproof sheet or bag. Such a covering must not prevent the gun being mounted for action immediately.

7. Ammunition, spare parts, and anti-gas apparatus will be inspected daily.

    The Gun Commander will be responsible that all anti-gas apparatus is always in position and in order.

8. The lock spring will never be left compressed.

    With the Vickers gun it is generally sufficient to half-load and then press the thumb-piece when mounting the gun at night. In order to open fire, it is only necessary to complete the loading motion and press the thumb-piece.

9. All dug-outs, emplacements and ammunition recesses belonging to the gun position must be kept clean and in good repair.

SPECIAL ORDERS FOR THIS GUN POSITION.

1. The S.O.S. signal is_____

2. Action on S.O.S._____

3. Action if enemy penetrates our front line_____

4.

5.

6.

Appendix I.—*continued.*

LIST OF STORES BELONGING TO THIS GUN POSITION

Article	Number	Remarks
Fighting Map ...		
Barrage Chart ...		
Intelligence Summary		
Mountings (pivot, box, wooden base, etc.) ...		
Mills Grenades ...		
Picks ...		
Shovels ...		
Refuse tin ...		
Sundries ...		

Date .. _ _____   *Machine Gun Officer.*

APPENDIX II.

TYPES OF MACHINE GUN EMPLACEMENTS.

(a)

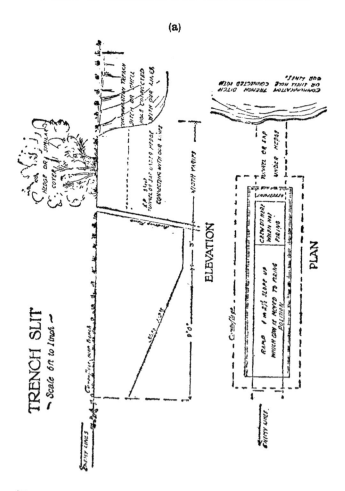

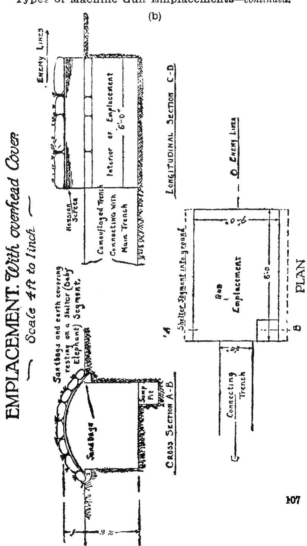

EMPLACEMENT. *With overhead Cover.*
Scale 4 ft to 1 inch.

LONGITUDINAL SECTION C-D

CROSS SECTION A-B

PLAN

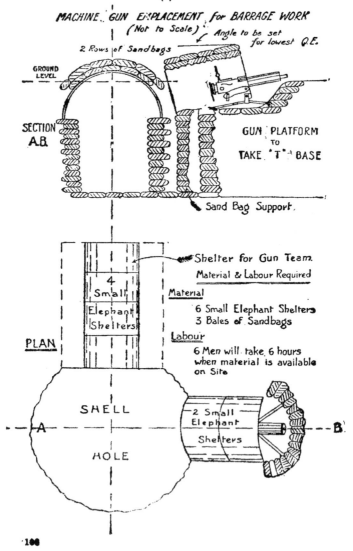

MACHINE. GUN EMPLACEMENT for BARRAGE WORK
(Not to Scale)   Angle to be set for lowest Q.E.

2 Rows of Sandbags

GROUND LEVEL

SECTION A.B.

GUN PLATFORM TO TAKE "T" BASE

Sand Bag Support.

Shelter for Gun Team.

Material & Labour Required

Material
  6 Small Elephant Shelters
  3 Bales of Sandbags

Labour
  6 Men will take 6 hours when material is available on Site

4 Small Elephant Shelters

PLAN

A — SHELL HOLE — B

2 Small Elephant Shelters

190

APPENDIX III.

A.—OFFENSIVE OPERATIONS.

Typical Communications of Rear Guns on a Brigade Front.

Forward Guns communicate through the Infantry Battalions in whose area they are operating.)

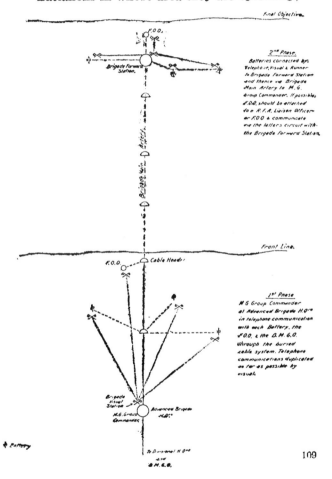

Appendix III.—*continued.*

B.—TRENCH WARFARE.

Typical Communications of Machine Guns on a Division Front.
(Forward sections communicate through the Infantry Battalions in whose area they are operating.)

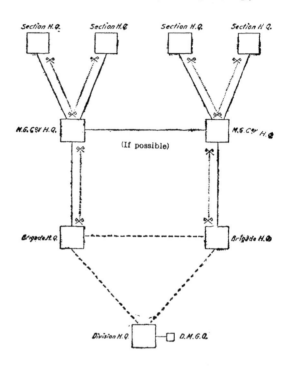

M G Lines _____
Infantry Lines ___ ___
Visual (if possible) . . ___ ✂

110

APPENDIX IV.

TABLE 1.—TANGENT ELEVATION, ANGLES OF DESCENT, DIMENSIONS OF CONES AND ZONES, &c. ·303 VICKERS GUN, MARK VII AMMUNITION.

1	2	3		4	5				6	
	Angle of Tangent Elevation.	Slope of Descent.		Height in yards of lowest shot below cr. of cone.	Dimensions in yards of horizontal beaten zones.				Dimensions of cones in yards.	
Range.					Width.		Length.		Width.	Height.
Yards.	Minutes.	In Minutes.	As a Gradient.		75 p.c.	90 p.c.	75 p.c.	90 p.c.	75 p.c.	75 p.c.
100	3	—	—	—	—	—	—	—	—	—
200	7	—	—	.7	.3	—	—	—	.3	—
300	11	—	—	1.0	.5	—	—	—	.5	—
400	16	15	One in 230	1.3	.7	—	—	—	.7	--
500	22	23	,, 149	1.7	.8	2.3	220	700	.8	1.5
600	28	32	,, 107	2.0	1.0	2.8	204	600	1.0	1.9
700	35	42	,, 82	2.3	1.2	3.3	188	525	1.2	2.3
800	43	54	,, 64	2.7	1.3	3.8	172	450	1.8	2.7
900	52	69	,, 50	3.0	1.5	4.3	156	375	1.5	3.1
1000	62	88	,, 39	3.3	1.7	5.0	140	300	1.7	3.6
1100	73	111	,, 31	4.0	2.0	6.0	126	270	2.0	4.1
1200	86	139	,, 25	4.7	2.3	7.0	112	240	2.3	4.5
1300	101	172	,, 20	5.3	2.7	8.0	98	210	2.7	4.9
1400	117	209	,, 16	6.0	3.0	9.0	84	180	3.0	5.2
1500	135	251	,, 14	6.7	3.3	10.0	75	160	3.3	5.4
1600	155	298	,, 12	7.8	4.0	11.3	70	150	4.0	5.8
1700	177	350	,, 9.8	8.0	4.7	12.7	70	145	4.7	7.2
1800	201	407	,, 6.5	8.7	5.3	14.0	70	140	5.3	8.3
1900	227	469	,, 7.3	9.3	6.0	15.3	70	135	6.6	9.6
2000	256	541	,, 6.4	10.0	6.7	16.7	70	130	6.7	10.9
2100	288	623	,, 5.5	13.3	8.0	18.0	74	140	8.0	13.4
2200	322	715	,, 4.8	16.7	9.3	19.3	78	150	9.3	16.2
2300	360	817	,, 4.2	20.0	10.7	20.7	82	160	10.7	19.5
2400	401	929	,, 3.7	25.0	12.0	22.0	86	170	12.0	23.2
2500	447	1052	,, 3.3	30.0	13.3	23.3	90	180	13.3	27.2
2600	496	1186	,, 2.9	35.0	16.7	25.0	100	190	16.7	34.5
2700	551	1332	,, 2.6	41.7	20.0	26.7	110	200	20.0	42.3
2800	610	1491	,, 2.3	48.3	23.3	28.3	120	210	23.3	52.1

Appendix IV.—continued.

TABLE 2 (A).   TRAJECTORY TABLE.
.303 VICKERS GUN, MARK VII AMMUNITION.

POINT DISTANT FROM GUN IN YARDS.

RANGE YARDS	200	300	400	500	600	700	800	900	1000	1100	1200	1300	1400	1500	1600	1700	1800	1900	2000
0																			
L.S.	·37	·10	·13	·17	2½	2·3	2·7	3·0	3·5	4·0	4·7	5·3	6·0	6·7	7·3	8·0	8·7	9·3	10·0

	2100	2200	2300	2400	2500	2600	2700	2800
L.S.	13·3	167	20·5	25·0	30·0	35·0	417	—

NOTES.

The table is divided into two parts, one below the zero line and the other above. That part below the zero line is the ordinary trajectory table; that part above and the words "positive" and "negative" are for use when determining clearance in Indirect Overhead Fire. See Section 10, Notes para. vii.

PART BELOW ZERO LINE.

1.—This table gives at any distance from the gun the height in yards of the centre of the cone ABOVE the line of sight. When used for clearance, line of sight is taken to be horizontal.

EXAMPLE.—At a range of 1900 yards, and at a distance of 1000 yards from the gun the centre of the cone is 48·3 yards above the line of sight.

2.—To find the height of the lowest shot above the line of sight SUBTRACT the figure in the line marked L.S. from the height of the trajectory.

EXAMPLE.—At a range of 1800 yards the lowest shot at 900 yards above the gun is 39 − 3 = 36 yards above the line of sight.

PART ABOVE ZERO LINE.

1.—This table gives at any distance from the gun the depth in yards of the centre of the cone BELOW a horizontal plane passing through the gun position. When using this table the range is not the range to the target, but is the quadrant angle on the gun converted to a range by Table 1, column 2.

EXAMPLE.—At a range of 800 yards, and at a distance of 1200 yards from the gun the centre of the cone is 15 yards below the horizontal plane through the gun position.

2.—To find the depth of the lowest shot below the horizontal plane passing through the gun position ADD the figure in the line L.S. to the height of the trajectory.

EXAMPLE.—At a range of 800 yards, the lowest shot at 1400 yards from the gun is 30 plus 6 = 36 yards below the horizontal plane through the gun position.

Appendix IV.—continued.

Table 2 (B).—Trajectory Table for Negative Quadrant Angles.
.303 Vickers Gun, Mark VII Ammunition.

Distance of Point from Gun in Yards.

Q.E. Mins.	500	600	700	800	900	1000	1100	1200	1300	1400	1500	1600	1700	1800	1900	2000
	.7	.9	1.0	1.2	1.3	1.4	1.6	1.7	1.9	2.0	2.1	2.3	2.5	2.6	2.7	2.9
-0	8.2	4.8	7.1	16.0	13.6	18.0	23.4	30.0	38.2	47.6	58.9	72.1	87.6	106	125	149
-25	6.8	9.2	12.9	15.8	20.2	25.3	31.7	39.1	47.6	57.6	69.7	83.7	99.6	118	139	163
-50	10.4	13.6	17.3	21.6	26.7	32.6	39.7	47.8	57.1	67.8	80.6	95.5	112	131	153	178
-75	14.1	17.9	22.4	27.4	33.2	39.8	47.8	56.5	66.6	78.0	91.6	107	124	144	167	192
-100	17.7	22.3	27.6	33.2	39.8	47.2	55.6	65.4	76.0	88.4	102	119	137	158	180	207
-125	21.3	26.8	32.7	38.0	46.4	54.5	63.6	74.0	85.5	98.5	113	130	149	171	194	221
-150	24.9	31.1	37.8	44.7	52.9	61.6	71.6	82.8	95.0	109	124	142	162	184	208	236
-175	28.5	35.4	42.9	50.5	59.5	68.9	79.6	91.5	104	119	135	154	174	197	222	250
-200	32.2	39.7	47.8	56.4	66.1	76.1	87.6	100	114	129	146	166	186	210	236	265
-225	35.5	44.1	52.9	62.2	72.7	83.4	95.6	109	123	139	157	177	199	223	250	279
-250	39.5	48.4	58.3	68.0	79.0	90.7	104	118	133	149	168	188	211	236	264	294
-275	42.8	52.8	63.3	73.8	85.6	98.0	112	126	142	159	179	200	224	249	277	308
-300	46.8	57.1	68.4	79.6	92.1	105	120	135	152	160	190	211	236	262	291	323
-325	50.0	61.5	73.2	85.2	98.6	113	128	144	161	180	201	223	248	275	305	
-350	54.1	65.8	78.3	91.2	105	120	136	152	171	190	212	235	261	288		
-375	57.2	70.2	83.4	97.0	112	127	144	161	180	200	223	246				
-400	61.3	74.5	88.5	103	118	134	152	170	189	210	234					
-425	65.0	78.9	93.6	109	125	142	160	179	199	220	244					
-450	68.6	83.2	98.7	115	131	149	168	189	208	230	255					
-475	72.2	87.6	104	120	138	156	176	196	218	240						
-500	75.9	92.1	109	126	145	163	184	205	227							
-525	79.5	96.5	114	132	151	170										
-550	83.1	101	119	138	158	178										

Notes.

1.—This table gives at any distance from the gun the depth IN YARDS of the centre shot of the cone below a horizontal plane passing through the gun position.

2.—It is for use when determining clearance over our own troops heads in indirect overhead fire.

3.—The line Q.E. = −5 means that at 1000 yards, for instance, each addition of 5 minutes to the Q.E. adds 1·5 yards to the depth of the trajectory.

Example.

Q.E. = −255 minutes; range = 1400 yards. Trajectory depth below horizontal plane = 149 plus 2 yards for each 5 minutes added above 250.

= 149 + (½ × 2) = 155.

Appendix IV.—continued.

Table 3 (A).—The Quadrant Angle in Minutes, knowing Range and V.I. .303 Vickers Gun, Mark VII. Ammunition,

Target ABOVE Gun.

Range to Target in Yards.

V.I. in Yards.	500	600	700	800	900	1000	1100	1200	1300	1400	1500	1600	1700	1800	1900	2000	2100	2200	2300	2400	2500	2600	2700	2800
(1 yd adds)	7	6	5	4	4	3	3	3	3	2	2	2	2	2	2	2	2	2	1	1	1	1	1	1
5	56	57	60	65	71	70	80	100	114	129	147	166	187	211	236	265	296	330	368	408	454	503	557	616
10	91	85	84	86	90	96	104	115	127	142	158	177	197	220	245	273	304	358	375	415	461	509	564	622
15	125	115	109	108	109	114	120	129	141	154	169	187	207	230	254	282	313	345	382	423	468	516	570	628
20	160	143	133	129	129	131	136	143	154	166	181	194	218	239	263	290	321	356	390	430	475	522	577	635
25	194	171	158	151	148	148	151	158	167	178	192	200	228	249	272	299	329	361	397	437	481	529	583	641
30	228	200	183	172	167	165	167	172	181	191	204	230	238	258	281	308	337	369	405	444	488	536	589	647
35	263	229	207	194	186	183	185	186	194	203	215	240	248	264	291	316	345	377	412	451	495	542	596	653
40	297	258	232	215	205	200	199	201	207	215	227	241	258	278	300	325	354	385	420	458	502	549	602	659
45	332	286	256	237	224	217	214	215	220	228	238	252	268	287	309	334	362	392	427	465	509	556	608	665
50	366	315	281	258	243	234	230	229	233	240	250	263	278	297	318	342	370	400	435	473	516	562	615	672
55	400	344	305	270	262	251	245	244	247	252	261	273	283	306	327	351	378	408	442	480	523	569	621	678
60	435	372	330	301	281	268	261	258	260	265	273	281	299	316	336	359	386	416	450	487	530	576	628	684
65	469	400	354	323	300	285	274	272	273	277	284	295	309	325	345	368	394	424	457	494	537	582	634	690
70	503	429	378	344	319	303	292	287	286	289	296	306	319	335	354	376	402	432	465	501	544	589	640	696
75	538	458	403	366	338	320	307	302	300	302	307	316	329	314	362	385	411	440	472	509	550	596	646	703
80	572	486	428	387	358	337	323	317	313	314	319	327	330	354	372	394	419	448	480	516	557	603	652	709
85	606	515	452	408	377	354	339	331	327	327	330	335	349	363	381	403	427	456	487	523	564	609	659	715
90	641	544	477	429	396	371	354	340	340	339	342	348	359	373	390	411	436	464	495	530	571	616	665	721
95	675	572	502	451	415	389	369	360	353	351	353	359	369	383	399	420	444	471	502	539	577	622	671	727
100	709	602	526	472	434	406	385	375	366	363	364	370	379	392	408	429	452	479	510	545	584	629	678	733

Notes.

1.—This table combines the angle of sight with the angle of tangent elevation, thereby producing the quadrant angle directly.

2.—It is used as follows:—Range = 1800 yards. Target 55 yards above gun. Quadrant elevation = 327 minutes.

3.—The top line where V.I = 1 yard is used as follows.—Example I: Range = 1800. V.I. = 57 yards. The quadrant elevation for range = 1800 and V.I. = 55 is 227 minutes. For each extra yard of V.I. the top line shows that 2 minutes must be ADDED. Therefore necessary quadrant angle is 227 plus (2 × 2) = 331 minutes.

Appendix IV.—continued.

TABLE 3 (B).—THE QUADRANT ANGLE IN MINUTES, KNOWING RANGE AND V.I.

·303 VICKERS GUN, MARK VII. AMMUNITION.

Target BELOW Gun.

Range to Target in Yards.

V.I. in Yards	500	600	700	800	900	1000	1100	1200	1300	1400	1500	1600	1700	1800	1900	2000	2100	2200	2300	2400	2500	2600	2700	2800
1	7	6	5	4	4	3	3	3	3	2	2	2	2	2	2	2	2	2	1	1	1	1	1	1
5	−12	−1	10	21	33	45	57	72	88	105	123	144	167	191	218	248	280	314	352	394	440	469	545	604
10	−47	−29	−14	0	14	28	42	57	76	92	112	133	157	182	209	239	272	306	345	387	433	483	538	593
15	−81	−58	−39	−22	−6	10	26	43	61	80	101	123	147	172	200	230	263	299	338	379	426	470	532	592
20	−116	−87	−64	−43	−25	−7	10	28	48	68	89	112	136	163	191	222	255	291	330	372	420	470	525	585
25	−150	−115	−88	−65	−44	−24	−6	14	35	55	78	101	125	153	182	213	247	283	323	365	413	463	519	579
30	−184	−144	−113	−86	−63	−41	−21	0	21	48	66	90	116	144	173	204	239	275	315	358	404	456	513	573
35	−219	−173	−137	−108	−82	−59	−37	−14	8	31	55	80	108	134	164	196	231	267	308	351	399	450	506	567
40	−253	−202	−162	−129	−101	−76	−52	−29	−18	19	43	69	99	124	155	187	222	259	299	344	392	443	500	561
45	−288	−230	−186	−151	−120	−93	−68	−43	−29	6	32	58	90	115	146	178	214	252	293	336	385	436	494	555
50	−322	−259	−211	−172	−139	−110	−83	−57	−31	−6	20	47	76	105	137	170	206	244	286	329	378	430	487	548
55	−357	−288	−235	−193	−158	−127	−99	−72	−45	−18	0	37	66	96	128	161	198	236	278	322	371	423	481	542
60	−391	−316	−260	−215	−177	−145	−115	−86	−58	−31	−14	26	55	85	119	153	189	228	270	315	364	416	474	536
65	−425	−344	−284	−237	−197	−161	−130	−100	−71	−43	−26	15	45	77	110	144	181	220	263	308	358	410	468	530
70	−460	−372	−308	−258	−216	−179	−146	−115	−84	−55	−37	5	35	67	101	136	173	212	255	301	351	403	462	524
75	−495	−401	−333	−280	−235	−196	−161	−129	−97	−67	−57	−6	25	57	92	128	166	206	248	294	344	397	456	518
80	−529	−430	−358	−301	−254	−214	−177	−144	−111	−79	−48	−17	15	48	82	119	158	199	240	287	337	391	449	512
85	−563	−459	−382	−323	−273	−231	−192	−158	−124	−92	−60	−28	5	38	73	111	149	191	233	280	330	384	443	506
90	−598	−488	−407	−344	−292	−248	−208	−172	−137	−104	−71	−39	−5	29	64	102	141	183	225	273	323	378	436	500
95	−632	−517	−431	−366	−311	−265	−223	−187	−150	−117	−83	−50	−15	19	55	93	132	175	218	266	316	371	430	494
100	−666	−545	−456	−387	−330	−282	−239	−200	−163	−129	−94	−60	−25	10	46	85	124	167	210	259	310	365	424	488

NOTES.

1.—This table combines the angle of sight with the angle of tangent elevation, thereby producing the quadrant angle directly.

2.—It is used as follows :—Range = 1000 yards. Target 55 yards below gun. Quadrant elevation = 128 minutes.

3.—The top line where V.I. = ¼ yard is used as follows :—EXAMPLE I. Range = 1900 yards. Target 57 yards below gun. The quadrant angle for range = 1900 and V.I. = 55 is 128 minutes. For each extra yard of V.I. the top line shows that 2 minutes must be SUBTRACTED. Therefore necessary quadrant angle is 128 − (2 × 2) = 124 minutes. EXAMPLE II. Range = 1300 yards, V.I. = 38 yards, Q.E. = 8 − (3 × 3) = − ¼ minute. EXAMPLE III. Range = 1100 yards, V.I. = 47 yards, Q.E. = − 68 − (2 × 8) = − 7¼ minutes.

115

Appendix IV.—*continued*.

Table 4.—Atmospheric Allowance (in minutes).

NORMAL RANGE.		1000	1100	1200	1300	1400	1500	1600	1700	1800	1900	2000	2100	2200	2300	2400	2500	2600	2700	2800		M.P.H. × 22 = FEET per SECOND.
	M.P.H.																				H.P.H.	
HEAD WINDS ADD — REAR WINDS DEDUCT.	5	0	1	1	1	2	2	2	2	3	4	5	6	7	8	10	12	15	17	22	5	90
	10	1	1	2	2	3	4	4	4	6	8	9	11	14	17	20	24	30	37	44	10	15
	15	1	2	3	3	4	6	6	6	9	11	13	17	24	27	30	37	44	58	67	15	90
	20	1	2	3	4	5	8	8	9	13	15	17	23	29	34	40	49	61	75	89	20	95
	25	1	3	4	5	6	10	10	12	16	19	24	29	33	43	50	61	76	92	112	25	30
	30	2	4	5	6	8	12	12	16	19	23	30	35	35	51	61	73	91	109	136	30	35
	35	3	4	6	7	11	14	14	19	24	27	35	40	50	59	70	87	107	119	167	35	

		1000	1100	1200	1300	1400	1500	1600	1700	1800	1900	2000	2100	2200	2300	2400	2500	2600	2700	2800		BELOW 30° DEDUCT.
BAROMETER ABOVE 30 ADD.	30·2	0	1	1	1	1	1	2	2	2	2	2	3	3	4	5	5	6	6	6	30·2"	
	30·4	0	1	1	1	1	1	2	3	4	4	4	5	5	7	7	8	10	9	10	30·4"	
	30·6	1	1	2	2	3	3	3	4	5	5	6	6	7	9	9	10	16	13	16	30·6"	
	30·8	1	1	2	2	3	4	4	5	7	7	7	8	9	11	11	12	22	15	22	30·8"	
	31·0	1	2	3	3	4	4	5	5	8	8	9	11	12	13	14	15	25	23	25	31·0"	

		1000	1100	1200	1300	1400	1500	1600	1700	1800	1900	2000	2100	2200	2300	2400	2500	2600	2700	2800		BELOW 60° ADD.
TEMPERATURE (FAH.)	65°	0	1	1	1	1	1	3	3	3	3	3	6	6	6	7	7	8	8	9	55°	
	70°	1	1	2	2	3	3	3	5	6	6	9	7	7	10	12	12	14	16	18	50°	
	75°	1	2	3	3	4	5	5	7	7	8	9	12	12	13	14	18	20	33	28	45°	
ABOVE 60° DEDUCT.	80°	2	3	4	4	5	6	6	9	11	11	15	16	16	18	20	24	30	41	36	40°	
	85°	2	3	5	6	7	8	8	11	13	13	18	20	24	22	25	30	36	48	44	35°	
	90°	3	4	6	7	8	9	9	13	16	17	21	24	27	31	35	36	41	55	53	30°	
	95°	4	4	7	8	10	11	11	16	19	20	24	27	33	36	40	48	49	60	62	25°	
	100°	5	5	8	9	11	12	13	18	23	23	28	33	33	41	45	54	55	73	70	20°	
	105°	5	6	9	10	12	15	16	20	26	26	31	40	40	45	50	55	63	78	80	15°	
	110°	6	7	9	11	13	16	18	23	28	28	35	44	44	56	56	63	68	85	88	10°	
	115°	7	8	10	12	13	17	20	25	31	31	37	49	49	63	63	74	74	92	98	5°	
	120°	8	9	11	13	14	17	23	26	35	35	43	56	56	70	63	81	81	99	106	0°	

NOTE.—Normal atmospheric conditions = still air. Barometer 30". Temperature 60°F. Convert Oblique Winds and thus get the equivalent Head and Rear Wind by Appx. 4, Table 5.

EXAMPLE:—Map Range 2400 yds. (QE.401'). Wind 15 M.P.H. "Head." Barom. 29·6" Temp. 50°F. To get corrected QE. =
(1) Find necessary allowance in column "Normal Range."
(2) Find necessary allowance for Head and Rear Wind 15 M.P.H. = +30'.
(3) Find allowance for Barom. 29·6" = –7'.
(4) Find necessary allowance for Temp. 50°F. = +10'.
(5) ADD 33' to 401' = 434' Corrected QE.
(6) +30' –7' +10' = +33'.

Appendix IV.—*continued.*

TABLE 5.—LATERAL WIND ALLOWANCES.

Range	Mild 10 M.P.H.		Fresh 20 M.P.H.		Strong 30 M.P.H.	
Yards	Yards	Minutes	Yards	Minutes	Yards	Minutes
500	1	5	1½	10	2	15
1000	3	10	6	20	9	30
1500	6	15	12	30	18	45
2000	12	20	24	40	36	60
2500	24	30	48	60	72	90

OBLIQUE WIND ALLOWANCES.

Angle of Wind with Line of Fire	Ratio of Wind affecting Elevation	Ratio of Wind affecting Direction
10° 20°	1	¼
30° 40°	¾	½
50° 60°	½	¾
70° 80°	¼	1

TABLE 6.—TIME OF FLIGHT.

Time of Flight in Seconds.	Distance Traversed in Yards.
1	600
2	1000
3	1300
4	1550
5	1775
6	1950
7	2100
8	2225
9	2350
10	2450
11	2550
12	2625
13	2700
14	2775
15	2840

All Figures represent Yards.

TABLE 7. SEARCHING REVERSE SLOPES.
.303 VICKERS GUN. MARK VII. AMMUNITION.

1	2	3	4	5	6	7	8	9	10	11	12	Gun Above or Below Crest	12	11	10	9	8	7	6	5	4	3	2	1
1950	1400	1630	1700	1650	1650	1650	1700	1800	1850	2000	2050	**0**	1900	1800	1700	1600	1500	1400	1400	1350	1300	1300	1300	1200
1350	1400	1550	1600	1650	1700	1750	1800	1850	1900	1950	2000	**10**	2050	2000	1930	1900	1850	1800	1750	1650	1600	1500	1400	1350
1400	1450	1550	1600	1650	1700	1750	1800	1900	1950	2000	2050	**20**	2000	1950	1900	1850	1800	1750	1650	1600	1550	1450	1300	1200
1500	1500	1600	1650	1750	1800	1800	1850	1900	1950	2000	2100	**30**	1950	1900	1880	1750	1650	1600	1550	1500	1450	1350	1250	1100
1500	1550	1650	1700	1750	1800	1800	1900	1950	2000	2050	2100	**40**	1900	1850	1800	1700	1650	1600	1500	1450	1400	1300	1150	
1500	1600	1700	1700	1800	1850	1900	1950	2000	2050	2100	2100	**50**	1900	1850	1790	1650	1550	1550	1450	1400	1350	1200		
1600	1650	1700	1750	1800	1850	1930	1950	2000	2050	2100	2150	**60**	1830	1800	1700	1600	1450	1450	1400	1350	1300			
1650	1650	1750	1750	1850	1900	1950	2000	2050	2100	2150	2150	**70**	1800	1750	1650	1550	1400	1400	1350	1300				
1650	1700	1800	1850	1900	1950	1950	2050	2100	2150	2150	2150	**80**	1750	1750	1650	1500	1400	1300	1250					
1700	1750	1800	1850	1900	1950	2000	2050	2050	2100	2150	2200	**90**	1750	1700	1600	1450	1300	1250	1150					
1750	1800	1850	1850	1950	1950	2000	2050	2100	2150	2150	2200	**100**	1700	1650	1550	1400	1200	1100						
1800	1850	1900	1900	1950	2000	2050	2100	2150	2150	2200	2200	**110**	1650	1600	1500	1350	1150							
1850	1850	1900	1950	2000	2000	2050	2100	2150	2200	2200	2200	**120**	1600	1550	1450	1300	1100							
1850	1900	1950	1950	2000	2050	2100	2150	2200	2200	2250	2250	**130**	1600	1550	1450	1250								
1900	1950	1950	1950	2050	2050	2100	2150	2200	2250	2250	2250	**140**	1550	1500	1400	1200								
1900	2000	2000	2050	2050	2050	2100	2150	2200	2250	2250	2250	**150**	1500	1450	1350	1150								
	2000	2050	2050	2100	2100	2150	2200	2200	2250	2300	2250	**160**	1450	1400	1300									
	2050	2100	2150	2150	2150	2200	2200	2250	2300	2300	2300	**170**	1400	1350	1250									
		2100	2150	2150	2200	2200	2250	2250	2300	2300	2300	**180**	1400	1350										
			2200	2200	2250	2250	2250	2300	2300	2300	2350	**190**	1350	1300										
				2250	2250	2250	2300	2300	2350	2350	2350	**200**	1300											

Gun below Crest.   Gun above Crest.

NOTES.

1.—The top horizontal line is the drop in yards in the first 100 yards beyond the crest. The horizontal line directly below it is the distance to measure back from the crest to find gun position.

Note.—The crest may be taken as being either the highest point of the ground, or, in the case of a flat-topped hill, the point at which a gentle slope changes to a more abrupt one.

2.—Example.—The ground drops 7 yards in 100, and assume also that the gun is below the crest. The left-hand side of the table must therefore be used. The table shows that for a drop of 7 yards we must go back 1900 yards from the crest. At this point, say, the gun position is found to be 90 yards below the crest. Final range, therefore, equals 2000 yards. Place the gun at this point.

3.—When the gun is in position, fire should be directed on the crest, elevation and direction being put on by any of the usual methods for indirect fire. In the example given above, the quadrant angle is that for a V.I. of 90 yards and a range of 2000 yards—i.e., 411 minutes. See Table 3 (A).

4.—Searching should be employed away from the crest, but it must be remembered that as the cone is beating falling ground the length of the zone will be very much increased; therefore the turns of the wheel should be few in number.

5.—If the final position is not suitable, the gun should be moved further away from—not nearer to—the crest.

6.—If it be desired to engage an area of ground which lies some distance back from the crest, without searching back from the crest itself, the position of the gun must be determined with reference to the crest as detailed above. Then the quadrant elevation necessary to hit the near limit of the ground to be searched must be put on in the usual way for indirect fire.

GRAPH FOR CALCULATING QUADRANT ELEVATION AND CLEARANCES.

(CURVES REPRESENT CENTRE SHOTS.)

DEPTH OF LOWEST SHOT BELOW CENTRE OF CONE AT VARIOUS DISTANCES FROM GUN.

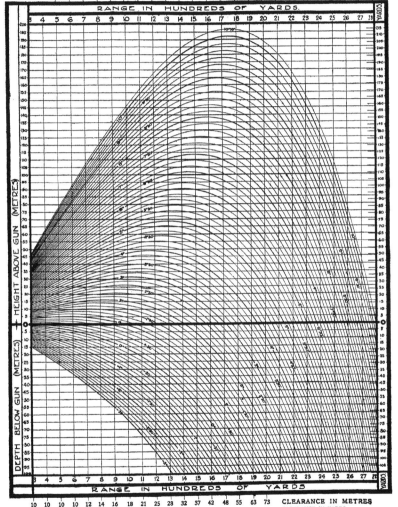

MINIMUM CLEARANCES REQUIRED AT VARIOUS DISTANCES FROM GUN.

How to Use the Graph.—To Find Q.E. : Take range and run up on vertical scale to height of target above or below gun. The curve cutting this point gives required Quadrant Elevation.

To Find Clearance.—Follow this curve along, and ascertain at what height it passes vertically above a point plotted to show distance and height (above or below gun) of own troops (or obstruction). This gives clearance in yards (right-hand scale), or metres (left-hand scale), from centre shot to ground.

Appendix V.—*continued.*

No. 2.

GRAPH of TRAVERSES, etc.
(IN YARDS OR METRES AND DEGREES)

The Angle is shewn by the diagonal line nearest to the point of intersection of the required Target Frontage line (vertical) and Hit (horizontal) Range line.

Note:— Both Target Frontage and Range must be taken in the same unit of measure: e.g. both in yards or both in metres.

SCALE for the conversion of OBLIQUE to equivalent FRONTAL TARGETS.
EXAMPLE:— Target 200' long at an angle of 150° to line of fire. The scale gives 45 so equivalent frontal target = 45 of 200' = 126"

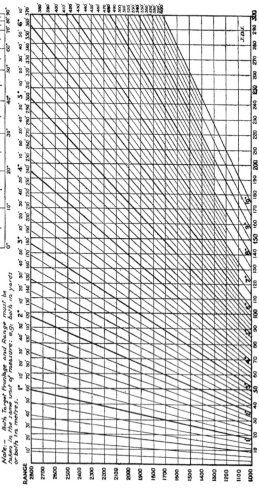

RANGE

TARGET FRONTAGE

J.D.H.

APPENDIX VI. No. 1.
INDIRECT OVERHEAD FIRE SHEET.

No..........M.G. Co.   No..........Section.   Date..............   Map used..............

ELEVATION									CLEARANCE							
Gun position	Map location	Target	Map location	Direction	Range to Target	Contours Gun / Target	V.I. + or V.I. −	Q.E. Table 3 (A) or 3 (B)	Range for Q.E. Table 1, Col. 1 and 2	Contour of own Troops	V.I. between Gun and own Troops	Range to own Troops	Trajectory Height Table 2 (A) or 2 (B)	Clearance obtained	Table of Safety Clearances	Grid bearing of Zero Line

Table of Safety Clearances:

600 – 11 ×
700 – 13 ×
800 – 15 ×
900 – 17 ×
1000 – 20 ×
1100 – 23 ×
1200 – 27 ×
1300 – 31 ×
1400 – 35 ×
1500 – 40 ×
1600 – 46 ×
1700 – 53 ×
1800 – 60 ×
1900 – 69 ×
2000 – 80 ×

Appendix VI.—continued. No. 2.
BATTERY CHART. D. Battery.

Ref.: 1/1000. Place: Date:

TASK:— Creeping Barrage, move forward to advanced battery position. D.2.

Composition No. 3 and 4 Sections No. M.G.C.	Frontage of Battery 70 yards.
Commanded by :	Grid Bearing to R.O. 31° 30'
Location of Directing Gun 7d. 50°. 23.	Zero Line 7d. 50. 23. through 6a 1.5.
No. of Directing Gun. No. 8	Grid Bearing of Zero Line 290° 30'

No. of Barrage	No. of Guns	Targets	Clock Times	Zero Time	Angle of Switch	Distribution Angle	Range	V.I.	Q.E.	Range to F.T. when Barrage lifts	Clearance when Barrage Lifts	Rate of Fire
A	1 to 8	2c 1.1. to 6a 1.5.		Z to Z+2	0°	50'	1800	−8x	3° 5'	1150x	39x	75 R.P.M.
B	1 to 8	1d 7.1. to 5b 7.5.		Z+3 to Z+5	1° 30' L	50'	2000	−10x	4°	1250x	58x	75 R.P.M.
C	1 to 8	1d 3.1. to 5h 3.5.		Z+6 to Z+8	3° L	40'	2200	−5x	5° 14'	1350x	87x	75 R.P.M.

REMARKS.

	1	9	3	4	5	6	7	8
A	5° 50' R	5° R	4° 10' R	3° 20' R	2° 30' R	1° 40' R	50' R	0°
B	4° 20' R	3° 30' R	2° 40' R	1° 50' R	1° R	10' R	40' L	1° 30' L
C	0° 40' R	1° R	20' R	20' L	1° L	1° 40' L	2° 20' L	3° L

This shews angle of Deviation from Zero Line for each gun. From this Table a Barrage Chart for each gun is compiled and issued to Gun Commanders.

To get parallel lines all guns 101° 30' Left. (NOTE:—The R.O. was in line with the guns).

GUN CHART.

No. 1 Gun.　　D. Battery.　　Gun Commander:—

Grid Bearing of Zero Line 290° 30'

No. of Barrage	Clock Time	Zero Time	Angle from Zero Line	Q.E.	Traverse	Rate of Fire
A		0 to 2	5° 50' R	3° 5'	2°	75 R.P.M.
B		3 to 5	4° 20' R	4°	2°	75 R.P.M.
C		6 to 8	1° 40' R	5° 14'	2°	75 R.P.M.

Chart of Concentration Points.

No. of Point	Angle from Zero Line	Q.E.	REMARKS
1	5° LEFT	6° 30'	Strong Point 5b 2.2.
2			
3			

APPENDIX VIII.

COMPASS TOWER.

Description.

The "Compass Tower," shown in the accompanying photograph has been designed for the purpose of laying the gun quickly and accurately on any given bearing by direct use of the Compass.

Experiments showed that the iron of the tripod did not affect the readings of a compass placed directly above the socket at a height of not less than 14 inches (the gun having been removed).

The pattern of tower illustrated is constructed of wood (mahogany). It is held upright by the crosshead joint pin to which it can be clamped by means of a wing nut. On the table forming the top of the instrument, a compass can be placed and held from moving by a leaf spring; the latter projects up through a hole in the table and presses the compass case against two round-headed screws.

The crosshead joint pin makes an angle of 90° with the axis of the bore, and the compass can be adjusted rapidly by means of an adjustable sight vane on the table, so that the line of sight through the compass is at right angles to the crosshead joint pin, and therefore parallel to the axis of the bore.

The overall length of this model is 16 inches; width $2\frac{1}{4}$ inches; weight 12 ounces.

Method of use.

To adjust: Lay the gun on some distant object, and tighten the traversing clamp securely. Remove the gun from the crosshead to a distance of at least three yards.

Place the compass tower in position on the crosshead, replace the crosshead joint pin, and clamp the tower in position by means of the clamping nut.

Place the compass on the table, and align it on the object by rotating the compass. Bring the sight vane of the compass tower into alignment with the hair line of the compass, and then clamp up the sight vane.

The compass tower will now be in adjustment.

To lay the gun on any magnetic bearing: Remove the gun from the vicinity of the tripod, and loosen the traversing clamp; place the compass tower on the crosshead, and align the hair line of the compass on the slit of the compass tower sight vane.

Rotate the crosshead until the required reading is seen on looking through the compass prism (or its equivalent).

Clamp up the traversing clamp; loosen slightly the clamping nut of the compass tower, and withdraw the crosshead joint pin. Remove the compass tower from the crosshead, and replace the gun which will now be pointing in the required direction.

123

Appendix VIII.—*continued.*

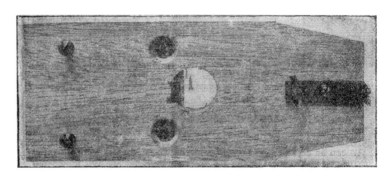

Fig. 1.—Plan of table of Compass Tower viewed from above.

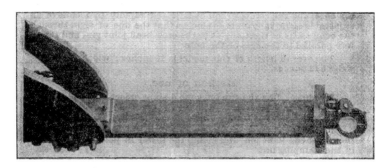

Fig. 2.—Perspective view of Compass Tower in position on the crosshead,
compass in position.

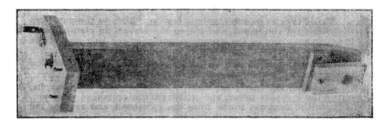

Fig. 3.—Perspective view of Compass Tower showing table, sight vane,
and securing clip.

APPENDIX IX.

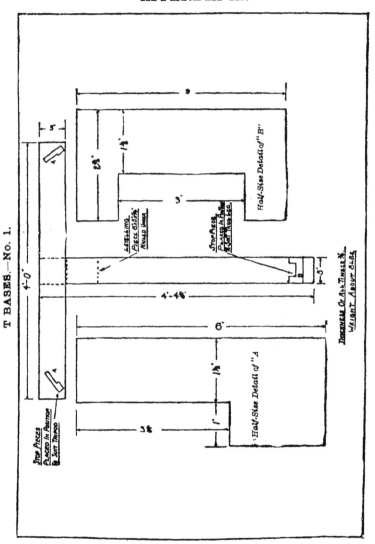

T BASES.—No. 1.

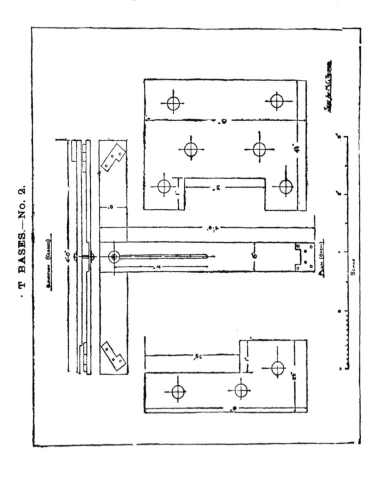

APPENDIX X.

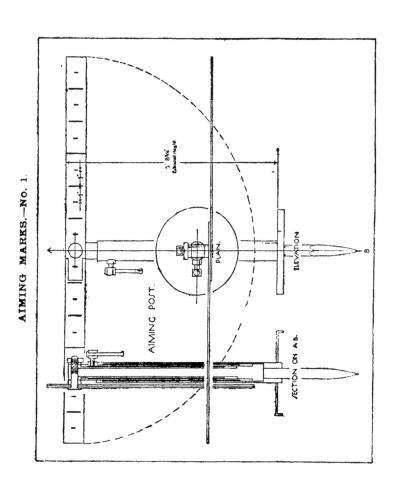

AIMING MARKS.—No. 1.

AIMING MARKS.—No. 1a.

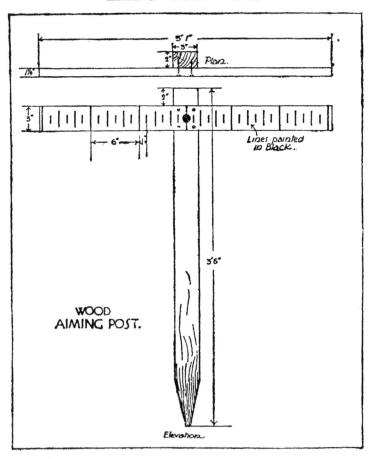

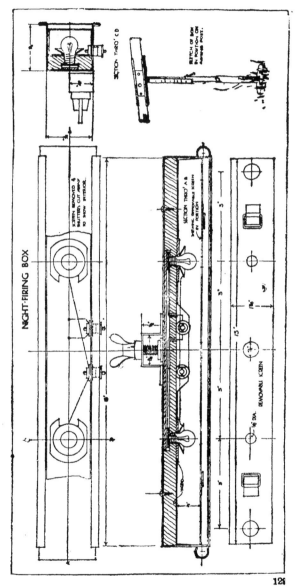

AIMING MARKS.—No. 2.

NIGHT-FIRING BOX

AIMING MARKS.—No. 3.

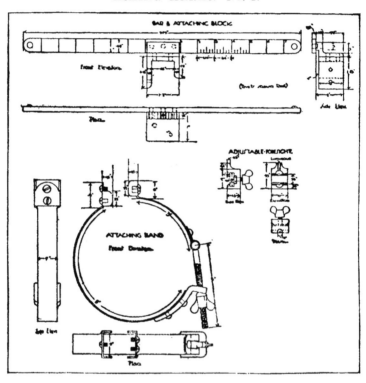

Appendix X.—*continued.*

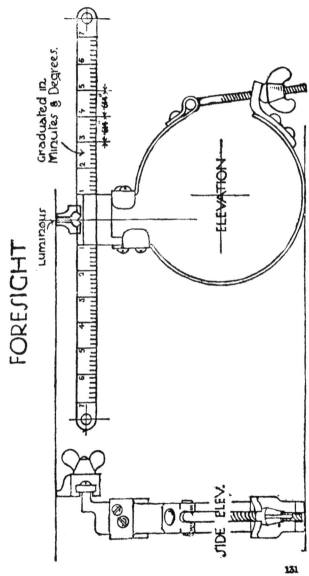

AIMING MARKS.—No. 4.

FORESIGHT

131

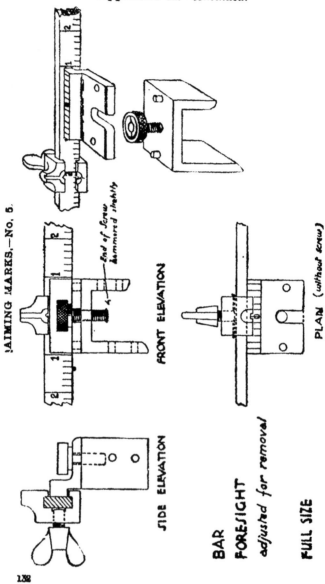

AIMING MARKS,—No. 5.

End of Screw hammered slightly

FRONT ELEVATION

SIDE ELEVATION

PLAN (without screw)

BAR

FORESIGHT

adjusted for removal

FULL SIZE

APPENDIX XI.

ADJUSTMENT OF THE MARK V. CLINOMETER.

(i.) Mount the gun with the socket upright.

(ii.) Set the clinometer to zero and place it on the gun.

(iii.) Without touching the gun move the elevating wheel until the bubble is central.

(iv.) Reverse the clinometer and place it in the same position on the gun.

(v.) If the bubble is still central the instrument is in adjustment.

If the bubble is not central, compare the clinometer with one which is in adjustment.   To do this—

(i.) Set the correct instrument to 2 deg.

(ii.) Place it on the gun and elevate the gun until the bubble is central.

(iii.) Replace the clinometer by the one which is out of adjustment and without moving the gun, set the instrument so that the bubble is central.

Take the reading.

E.g.   Suppose it is 2 deg. 10 min.

Then the instrument has a positive error of 10 min., and 10 min. must be added to any Q.E. before using the instrument to place elevation on the gun.

Again, if the reading is 1 deg. 50 min., then the error is negative and 10 min. must be subtracted from any Q.E. before using the instrument to place elevation on the gun.

In either case the error should be recorded on a piece of paper which should be pasted inside the clinometer case, until such time as the instrument can be adjusted.

No attempt should be made by companies to adjust the Mark V. clinometer, as the adjusting screws are very delicate and the adjustment should be done in workshops.

APPENDIX XII.

CARE OF MACHINE GUNS IN FROSTY WEATHER.

1. Not more than about 5 pints of water should be put into the barrel casing, and 20 per cent. of glycerine will prevent it from freezing quickly. In extremely hard weather, if the gun has to be exposed, experience has proved that 2½ pints of water plus 2½ pints of pure or residue glycerine is necessary. A drawback, however, to the large proportion of glycerine is that if fire is sustained until the mixture boils very bad fumes are given off. If the gun is used in a covered emplacement these fumes have more effect upon the team than the fumes given off by cordite.

2. Working parts should be slightly oiled with a lightly oiled rag. If firing is sustained oil must be applied to all frictional parts.

3. Guns should be wrapped in blankets, sandbags or rope, etc., and kept near braziers or in men's dug-outs or close to the body till required. If none of these courses is possible, the recoiling portions should be frequently worked, or single shots fired and the lock be changed at interals, the spare lock being kept in a clean pocket close to the body.

4. A proportion of ammunition should, if possible, be kept warm and changed at intervals.

5. If possible, some oil should be kept warm for use if firing is prolonged.

6. Should the water in the barrel casing become frozen solid, on the gun being fired the barrel will probably not recoil far enough to work the gun and will remain back. To remedy this, pull the crank handle on to the roller, then bring it back to a vertical position and force the barrel to the front, pulling the belt if necessary; let the crank handle return to the check lever and fire the gun. This should be repeated until the barrel recoils correctly.

7. If a gun is exposed in extremely hard weather, fuzee and other springs become brittle, and lose their quickness. Fuzee springs should be lightened, as the frost tends to increase their weight.

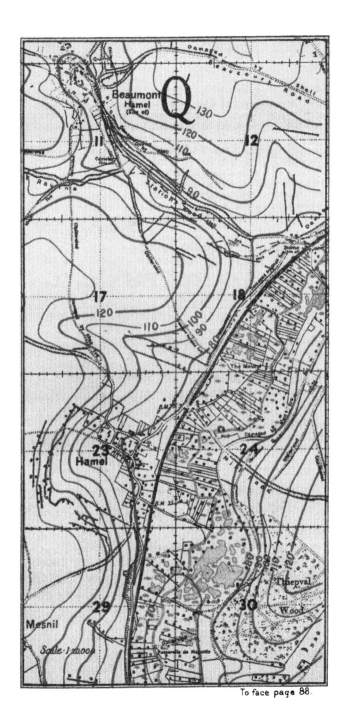

To face page 88.

APPENDIX VII.

FIGHTING MAPS.

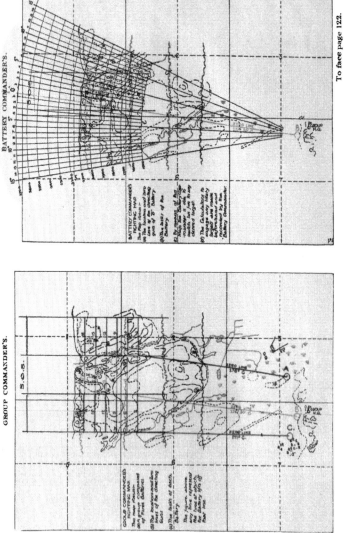

GROUP COMMANDER'S.

BATTERY COMMANDER'S.

S.O.S.

To face page 122.